Anglican Essays

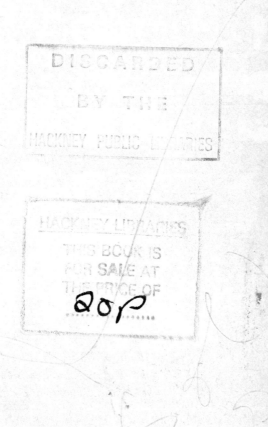

# Also by C. H. Sisson

### POETRY

*The London Zoo*
*Numbers*
*Metamorphoses*
*In the Trojan Ditch*
collected poems and selected translations
*Anchises*
*Exactions*
*Selected Poems*

### FICTION

*An Asiatic Romance*
*Christopher Homm*

### ESSAYS AND CRITICISM

*The Spirit of British Administration*
*Art and Action*
*English Poetry 1900–1950: an assessment*
*The Case of Walter Bagehot*
*David Hume*
*The Avoidance of Literature: collected essays*

### TRANSLATIONS

*Verses and Perversions of Heine*
*The Poetry of Catullus*
*The Poetic Art* (Horace)
*The Poem on Nature* (Lucretius)
*Some Tales of La Fontaine*
*The Divine Comedy of Dante*

# Anglican Essays

## C. H. SISSON

Carcanet Press

MANCHESTER

First published in Great Britain in 1983
by the Carcanet Press
208 Corn Exchange Buildings, Manchester M4 3BQ
Copyright © 1983 C. H. Sisson
SBN 85635 456 2

The publisher acknowledges the financial assistance
of the Arts Council of Great Britain

# Acknowledgments

Acknowledgement is due to the editors of the following journals: *The London Review of Books* where 'The Company he Keeps' (6-19 Aug 81), 'Public Schools' (1 Feb - 3 March 82) and 'The Politics of David Hume' (15 Apr - 5 May 82) first appeared; *The Times Literary Supplement,* where 'A Viewpoint on the Book of Common Prayer' (7 Dec 79), 'Poetry and Sincerity' (12 Sept 80), 'The Alternative Service Book' (14 Nov 80), 'Fairfax's Tasso and the Seventeenth Century' (20 Nov 81) and 'Richard Baxter' (6 Aug 82) first appeared; *the Spectator,* where 'A Gentle Warning' (2 May 81), 'Notes on Church and State' (1 Aug-5 Sept 81), 'The Reverend Member? (13 Feb 82) and 'The Archbishop's Travels' (10 April 82) first appeared; and *the Salisbury Review* where 'Richard Hooker and the "Ecclesiastical Polity"' first appeared. 'A Word of Apology' and 'Christian Sobriety' first appeared in *P.N Review 16* and *P.N Review 30* respectively.

Typesetting by Anneset, Weston-super-Mare, Avon
Printed in Great Britain by Short Run Press, Exeter

# Contents

# Introductory Note

THE disasters which have overtaken the Church of England, in recent years, are of more far-reaching consequence than is usually supposed. There are of course those who do not know that there have been disasters and these include, alas, many at present prominent in the Church. But for others, whether members of the Church or outside it, who know enough of history and literature – contemporary as well as past – the relegation of the Book of Common Prayer, the retreat from the claim to be the English Church, the concern with mere congregations instead of with the whole population, the distracting preoccupation with the Anglican and Roman internationals and political ambitions, are marks of a disorientation in which more is being lost than an ecclesiastical organization.

The subject is what is called *cultural,* in all the senses of that unsatisfactory term. If the ecclesiastical authorities say they are not interested in such matters, so much the worse for them as well as for us. It is in any case a subject of many ramifications – political, social and literary – and all the essays in this book do is to look tentatively at a few aspects of some of them. There is work for a generation in tracing the consequences of what has happened. The earliest of my pieces here reprinted was written in December 1979 at the request of the then editor of the *Times Literary Supplement,* John Gross, as one of the series of *Viewpoints,* by various hands, that he initiated; it deals with reactions to the petition in favour of the Book of Common Prayer organized by Professor David Martin and published in *Poetry Nation Review* (PNR 13, *For Cranmer and King James*). Other essays followed as other aspects of the changes of attitude in the

Church of England came to my notice, or as I found myself going back to some of the older Anglican writers whom I had found illuminating in the past. The result is a book in which the topics range from Richard Hooker and the 'Ecclesiastical Polity' to public schools and the Archbishop's travels.

Because those who signed David Martin's petition have often been accused of being little better than intellectuals – and because I have more recently distanced myself from the Church – perhaps I should add that I have in my time been a churchwarden in two parishes in different parts of the country, so am not unacquainted with the practical minutiae of parish life.

I should like to thank the editors concerned for permission to reprint these essays.

C H S

# Richard Hooker and the *Ecclesiastical Polity*

IT is the temper of Hooker, more than any particular doctrine expounded in *Of the Laws of Ecclesiastical Polity*, which gives him his place as the wisest among the Fathers of the post-Reformation English Church. His gentleness, his reasonableness as against all the exclusiveness of fanaticism, his determination not 'loosely through silence' to allow things 'to pass away as in a dream' but to carry the past with him into the future – these are the qualities which, until recently, marked the course of the central stream of Anglicanism. Without closing his mind to what had happened, or was happening, in other times and places, Hooker was intent on what he saw as the needs of the England of his own time, and it was this comprehensiveness, combined with his acute consciousness of local affairs, which made him the classic apologist of *the* Church of *England*: not a sect, but the historic heir of the mediaeval church; not a world-wide federation of theological opinion, like contemporary Anglicanism, but the one Sun seen, as it were, through the mists of this island – the only way it can in truth be seen, from this perspective. Not for nothing was he accused, by a contemporary of his own, of preaching 'that the assurance of what we believe by the word of God is not so certain as that which we perceive by sense' – an accusation which he characteristically sought to explain rather than to deny.

Hooker was born in 1553 or 4 in Devon, a county which, as Izaak Walton appropriately reminds readers of the *Life* (1665), 'furnished this nation with Bishop Jewel, Sir Francis Drake, Sir Walter Raleigh, and many others, memorable for their valour and learning'. He was thus a small child while, during Mary's reign, Protestants were being roasted at Smithfield and elsewhere. These horrors had, certainly, a profound effect on the attitudes of the rising generation, and contributed greatly to the popular impetus of Elizabeth's reign. A curious document of 1559 is Thomas Bryce's *Compendious Register in Metre* of those 'tormented and cruelly burnt within England, since the death of our famous Kyng of immortall memory Edwarde the Sixte' – a production which preceded Foxe's prose *Book of Martyrs* by several years. Month by month, from June 1555, through the terrible years 1555, 1556, 1557, 1558, to November of that last year when relief came in the form of the young Queen Elizabeth, Bryce records by name and place those who died, often ending his six-line stanzas with the name of a martyr, and always with the name of the Queen, as

> When Jone Polley was put to death...

or

> When Wade at Dartford died the death...

or

> When Jone Beche, widow, was done to death
> We wisht for our Elizabeth.

They had her at last, six days after the last of these Marian victims died. No wonder Bryce concludes:

> Pray we, therefore, both night and day,
> For her highnes, as we be bounde:
> Oh Lorde, preserve this branch of bay,
> And all her foes with force confounde;
>    Here long to lyve, and after death
>    Receyve our Queene Elisabeth.

The practical moral was the need for unity of religion, for the whole kingdom, under what could not fail to be, comparatively speaking, a benign monarch; and this, after all, is the subject of Hooker's great work, as it was one of the main domestic concerns of Elizabeth's reign. If the cloud of heresy charges was removed by the advent of Elizabeth, the political threat implicit in religious differences remained. It was in 1570 that the Pope excommunicated Elizabeth and released her subjects from their allegiance as far as in him lay – which was happily not very far. If this were not enough, Protestant fears were revived by 'the Massacre at Paris', as Marlowe called it – the murder of five or ten thousand Huguenots in Paris and other French cities on St Bartholomew's Day, 1572.

At this time Hooker was a young man of eighteen or nineteen, an age when he is unlikely to have been unimpressed by such events. The defeat of the Armada came when he was in his mid-thirties, and it removed the fear of foreign invasion, so giving solidity to Hooker's vision of an England in which Church and State lived as one, without either yielding to the other any part of its proper authority. There was not to be 'any man of the Church of England but the same man is also a member of the commonwealth; nor any man a member of the commonwealth, which is not also of the Church of England'. That was a version of mediaeval theory, brought up to date in a manner which implicitly discarded the Pope's pretensions to determine whether the Queen's subjects should be loyal to her, and in effect cut off from the commonwealth those who toyed with such errors. It is this disposition of things, and not any assertion about theological errors in the Roman Church, which has formed the basis of the various restrictions on the civil status of members of the Roman communion. The removal of these disqualifications by the series of Catholic Emancipation Acts had to await a time when the Pope's power to dispense people of their civil duties had become less widely credible.

To a generation which had faced the threat from Spain the need for loyalty to the crown needed no elaboration. In his discussion of the relations of Church and State, Hooker is largely preoccupied with a domestic problem, that of justifying the Royal Supremacy in ecclesiastical matters as against Puritans who thought themselves too holy to be meddled with. These apologetics were, however, in their nature also part of the argument for the validity of the English Church as against the Romans who continued to advance whatever objections they could think of. The Church in Hooker's view was not vitiated by the fact that every sort of ecclesiastical regulation was not in the hands of clerics. With a Christian monarch in a Christian commonwealth, how could that be? The Church was not only the clergy. The contention that supreme power in ecclesiastical causes must rest with the domestic clergy was merely a variant of the superstition that it must rest with the Bishop of Rome. Hooker's view of this matter rests fundamentally on his belief in reason and reasonableness, in 'the benefit of keeping the Law which reason teacheth' and 'the natural finding out of Laws by the light of Reason' which he had to advance against the crude inspirationalism of the more extreme Puritans, and the assertions of those who imagined that all light was to be extracted from the Scriptures. This reasonableness extended to and was one of the foundations of Hooker's view of kingship. He was as little appalled as Proudhon by the thought that a right may be established by conquest: 'For it is God who giveth victory in the day of war'; the facts spoke for themselves, one might say. Without order there is no public society; so, 'unto kings by human right, honour by very divine right, is due', as tribute was due to the Emperor Tiberius. The claim to a moral superiority over governments, made from their different points of view by Rome and by extreme Puritans, is not one that Hooker could entertain. In a Christian country, the civil and religious body were one, as the same man might be both schoolmaster and physician. 'When we oppose the Church therefore and the commonwealth in a Christian society, we mean by the commonwealth that society with relation to all the public affairs thereof, only the matter of true religion excepted; by the Church, the same society with only reference unto the matter of true religion, without any other affair besides.'

The problem Hooker poses, in relation to the affairs of our own time, is how such a view may be relevant in a state in which it can in no wise be claimed that every member of the commonwealth is a member of the Church, and vice versa. It is not to be supposed that, in mediaeval societies, the mass of the population was any more *christianized* than they are in England at present; if one takes as a criterion contemporary pronouncements, whether Papal or Protestant, on public affairs, they were in many respects less so. Still one cannot deny the growing dissociation, from the eighteenth century onwards, between Christian dogmatics and public institutions. Hooker had considered the position of the Church in relation to pagan society; there was the example of the Roman Empire before Constantine. Indeed he distinguished three positions: the first, 'under the dominions of infidels', where Church and State were, he said, 'two societies independent'. The second position was that of 'those commonwealths where the bishop of Rome holdeth sway'; there, church and commonwealth were one but the Pope divided them 'into two diverse bodies' and claimed the upper hand over 'any civil prince'. 'Thirdly... within this realm of England' the case was different again; the pattern was 'God's own ancient elect people' – the Old Testament pattern – where 'the self-same people' were 'whole and entire... under one chief Governor, on whose supreme authority they did all depend'.

Such a pattern is bound to be offensive in our present society – to our modern Puritans, who think the state unsanctified; to Jews, who regard the pattern as their copyright; to Roman Catholics, who want to give part of their allegiance abroad; in general, to all who believe in the sovereignty of public opinion, however mysteriously ascertained. A constitutional democracy does go some way to providing a solution, for it ensures the dissolution of any theocratic pattern of government. The adjustments are less than perfect, and the problem of relations between Church and State remains. The Roman church's claims to civil supremacy – already more than distasteful to Dante – remain, though now much muted, and operating not directly on governments but on the opinions of voters. The notion of the Pope's power to divide the *de facto* society into 'two diverse bodies' is strictly intolerable; it contradicts the assumptions of democracy. So is the notion of the right of any national church to regard itself as irresponsible in relation to the state; like the Roman church, it can only assemble opinions. Moreover, since the post-Christian society is not identical with 'the dominion of infidels', but is indeed a society in which Christians and non- or post-Christians have to get on side by side, as part of the same political body, supremacy in all practical matters has in the last analysis to be accorded to the state. There is a strong argument for saying that all collective opinions by churches on political matters are out of place, and that the only proper rôle left to them is to instruct their own members so that those members can exercise their several judgments in accordance with their consciences, and so play their individual parts in the state. There should be no question of special rights or privileges for churches – no rights, that is to say, which may not be accorded to non-religious organizations within the state. Some in the Church of England have lately been dreaming that if they withdrew from the historic position of the Establishment, they could be recognized as a special and sanctified body, with prophetic functions. This is a delusion. What would happen would be claiming, within the less protected area of the national authority, the kind of disruptive power Rome has traditionally claimed from a safer distance and its own temporal territory.

One can see new variants of Rome's ancient political game being played for an indefinite time to come, but the character of the game was changed entirely once she could no longer speak authoritatively to princes but seek only to influence opinion. The delusion of grandeur remains, but the many-headed people has become the master, in relation to such practical matters as the Pope could hope to influence outside his own geographical dominion. It may take a long time for this change to be effectively understood in the Vatican, but from the point of view of the national state the perspectives are clearer. The revolution which emerged at the Reformation is irreversible; there may in some future be a world government, but it will not be that of Rome. It could only be a political government which would accept the division of its authority with no better grace than have the national governments which have followed the destruction of the old Catholic monarchies. Meanwhile the national governments all base their claims to authority – in such terms as suit their several situations – on the whole body of their people. Individuals, to be sure, are free to consult their deity or his accredited agents, but governments no longer do so. In this matter as in so many others Hooker was remarkably long-sighted. That is not to say that he thought at all in terms acceptable in a modern democracy, but he understood that, whatever the constitutional arrangements in a state, it was 'a thing most true, that kings, even inheritors, do hold their right to the power of dominion, with dependency upon the whole entire body politic over which they have rule as kings'. The king is greater than the individual, but less than the whole society, *major singulis, universis minor.* As Bracton had said in the thirteenth century, the king should not be subject to any man, but to God and the law. The language is hardly of our time, but the radical meaning, as to the ultimate responsibility, and the limitations, of government, is much what we now approve, whatever developments it has undergone at the hands of Locke and his successors.

There are aspects of Hooker's reading of politics which are less generally understood, and which have been less taken up by those who have come after him. We should be apt to say that 'everyone has some religion' – for since Rousseau we have thought of such things very much in personal terms, as a matter of private thoughts and sentiments. For Hooker, 'every *body politic* hath some religion' – as was evident enough in his time; 'the Church that religion which is only true'. He was concerned with the society which was broadly Christian, which had 'true religion in the gross', and never mind the refinements. Such a society was the church – at once church and state, if one is to distinguish what he regarded as its two aspects; 'first united in some public form of regiment, and secondly distinguished from other societies by the exercise of the Christian religion'. For us churches are, politically, collections of private consciences, and we admit differences between them as between individuals, even though this is in contradiction with both the Church's and ordinary non-religious notions as to the universality of truth. It is arguable that no society can live long on such terms. It may be said that it involves a sleight of hand. For in such a situation, what are we to say of the religion of the body politic? That Hooker was wrong, and that the body politic has no religion? Or that it has a religion which is no longer that of the churches? If the former supposition is more plausible, in terms of contemporary prejudice, the latter is more likely, historically. Hooker looked back to the Old Testament world in which only Israel 'had the truth of religion, and was in that respect the Church of God', and in which other kingdoms had other religions. We look around on a world in which the governments of even 'Christian' countries discreetly make no appeal to the Christian religion, but to a system of 'rights' which they hope will prove more eirenic.

The Church of England, it sometimes appears, cannot too quickly get rid of the traces of Christendom still extant in our Constitution – a Christian monarchy and the two ecclesiastical establishments. It appears to have lost all faith in its mission as *the* historic church in this land, capable of infusing the whole society with the truth, yet that is its *raison d'être*. It makes loving signals to other ecclesiastical groups, but for the *res publica* it prefers that uncertain and as yet not fully formulated religion which the state has adopted as of necessity. The tendency towards disestablishment, which has been so marked in the Church of England in recent years, is a recession not only from the state but, so far as public affairs are concerned, from Christianity. One could understand a Church of England which aimed at reconciliation with dissenters, including Romans, in order to reconstitute, no doubt in some far future, a portion of Christendom. The abandonment of England, in favour of a retreat into individual quietism and participation in international gangs of opinion on this and that, is surely a betrayal. Such a point of view has always been that of those sects for whom the public welfare, and publicly acknowledged reason, meant nothing, and a sectarian future in a pagan state is all that we are now asked to look forward to.

The present generation of ecclesiastical conspirators do not, assuredly, hear the voice of George Herbert addressing *The British Church:*

> I joy, deare Mother, when I view
> Thy perfect lineaments and hue
>     Both sweet and bright.
> Beautie in thee takes up her place,
> And dates her letters from thy face,
>     When she doth write.

Neither, apparently, do they hear the voice of Richard Hooker.

# Christian Sobriety

THE near extinction of the Church of England, between the parliamentary ordinance for taking away the Book of Common Prayer in 1645 and the Restoration of 1660, had several important consequences. It profoundly affected the character of the settlement of 1662, and made for the touch of intolerance which troubled church and state for long enough after that date. There are two sides to this. There are the theological considerations, which make it inevitable that catholicity in theory should result in a certain exclusiveness in practice, and there are the considerations of civil peace, which must result in a pressure for a comprehensiveness possible only with a minimal dogmatic. To speak of the difficulties encountered by Roman and domestic non-conformists as a 'touch of intolerance' only may seem an outrage, but if one thinks of the Revocation of the Edict of Nantes, or the position of Protestants in Spain or Italy, it was no more. England in the late seventeenth century, and in the eighteenth century, was relatively 'the land of the free', in ecclesiastical as in other matters, as was recognized by other visitors besides Voltaire.

Even before the execution of Archbishop Laud, in 1645, there was a solid opinion in favour of comprehension and tolerance and with an eye on civil peace. Yet in 1642, when *The Holy State* was first published, Thomas Fuller was still too near the administrative unity of the mediaeval church, and its successor the national church, to think of 'voluntary private meetings' for religious purposes as being other than suspect. He was 'not peremptory but conjectural in doubtful matters. Not forcing others to his own opinions but leaving them to their own liberty'. But what are 'doubtful matters'? The field has extended since then beyond anything even the most liberal could have thought possible. By the time Fuller had had occasion for his *Good Thoughts in Bad Times* (1645) and *Good Thoughts in Worse Times* (1647) and had come to his *Mixt Contemplations in Better Times* (1660), he thought that the sects should 'have a toleration... and be permitted peaceably and privately to enjoy their consciences both in opinions and practices'; he hoped that so they would 'blush themselves out of their former follies, and by degrees cordially reconcile themselves to the Church of England'. For the Old Testament parallel remained: 'England hath but one Isaac or legitimate religion of the church, namely the protestant, as the doctrine thereof is established in the Thirty-nine Articles.' It was an aspiration rather than a practical programme, yet it was practical enough for the Church of England, with all its internal differences, to maintain its predominance until recent time, when the predominance has gone, not to any other form of Christianity, but to a lay conscience which may be half-Christian or post-Christian, but is anyway civic rather than ecclesiastical.

The truth is, that any articulated creed is widely acceptable only at the instance of a political authority, and indeed the basic Nicene creed (AD 325) owed its existence to the Emperor Constantine. The continuance in succeeding centuries of a Roman administration claiming to be distinguished in kind from the less educated polities with which it overlapped, has obscured this fact, but the maintenance of anything like theological uniformity has always depended on political power in the crudest sense of the term. The burning of heretics was a lay function, and the handing over of misbelievers to the civil arm while the Church washed her hands, is a ruse which takes nobody in once the right of the civil power to commit such outrages has been questioned. Once that stage has been passed, all closely-defined religion becomes sectarian, and the more liberty of conscience is allowed the more this becomes evident, for religion becomes in effect a matter of choice. The language of absolutism remains, above all in the Roman church, the most conservative, the most bureaucratic, and politically the most wary, with many features of a type of monarchy so long forgotten that people hardly recognize it for what it is. But for Romans as for the rest of the world, any degree of democratic sophistication in the civil state threatens the discipline of the Church, and brings the status of belief nearer to that of opinion.

Already, in the seventeenth century, the refinements of religious belief, the matters of doctrine which separate the churches, were losing their status as matters of fact. The internalization of religion accelerated by the Reformation meant the approximation of religious to political liberty, if not indeed the identification of the two forms. There is a sense in which martyrdom is a political rather than a religious phenomenon. The Protestant martyrs under Mary died because the state maintained its right to determine what people thought about religious matters. The Roman priests who were hanged under Elizabeth died as the agents of a foreign power, in effect for treason, a crime unlikely to be widespread under any ordinarily satisfactory government. This was an advance, so far as the internal peace of the kingdom was concerned, and saved innumerable lives. The claim for freedom of conscience in religious matters had still to be made, but it became less serious, in the ordinary sense of the term, once it was perceived not to be a matter of life and death. That is not to say that it was not the subject of noisy claims and counter-claims, but the noise and the extent of the dissidence is a phenomenon of psychological relief at the removal of intolerable pressures. The threat of hell-fire was less intimidating than that of the fires of Smithfield. The battles of persuasion and counter-persuasion themselves then became something peaceable persons sought to mitigate.

The many egotistical follies enacted in the name of religion could not be argued into submission, or even into reasonableness, nor could they be laughed out of existence, though this relatively new remedy was attempted, mainly by people whose opinions were more or less set and superficial, and who already looked upon the relatively recently established national church as the good old cause no one should meddle with. After the disaster sealed by the death of the king in 1649, more subtle and more religious minds took another turn, prompted by what they saw as the necessities of the times and partly no doubt by their own necessities. Thomas Fuller, whose temperament was benign and practical and who was more given to common sense that to refinements of argument, and Jeremy Taylor who was possessed of much greater flexibility of mind and, it must be supposed, to a much more intense internal religious life, turned their attention away from the public brawls, whether theological or political, towards the pacification of individual conduct. Amidst the welter of arguments, what is called practical Christianity, then as now, was no doubt the only thing which seemed convincing to the ordinary parishioner, however inadequate it might seem to more refined spirits. The great classic of Anglicanism produced by this new orientation is the *Holy Living* of Jeremy Taylor, with its sequel, *Holy Dying* (1650-51).

Although *Holy Living* was intended for ordinary Christians and was widely read by people who made no special profession of devotion, it contains sections on fasting, keeping festivals and prayer which supposes an attention to these practices which would probably seem fastidious, in our day, to all but a few. Yet the tone even in these sections is of an uncontroversial practicality. 'Fasting, if it be considered in itself... is a duty nowhere enjoined or counselled...' There is no scrupulosity; 'the help which fasting gives to prayer, cannot be served by changing flesh into fish, or milk meats into dry diet; but by turning much into little, or little into none at all...' Of prayer: 'nothing is lost, while words are changed into matter, and length of time into fervency of devotion'. 'Of Christian Religion' – in general – forms only the forth and final chapter of the book, the first three being given respectively to 'Consideration of the general instruments and means serving to a holy life', 'Of Christian sobriety' and 'Of Christian Justice'. There is no escaping the ordinary business of life and making up for it in religion. Conduct is the first matter for attention. The fourth chapter itself begins thus: 'Religion in a large sense doth signify the whole duty of man, comprehending in it justice, charity and sobriety: because all these being commanded by God they become a part of that honour and worship which we are bound to pay him.' It is, and rigorously, the religion of common life, from which one is not to be excused on any higher pretext; and it is for this reason, no doubt, that the book was taken so much to heart by generations of English people.

Section I of chapter 1 is on 'The first general Instrument of Holy Living, Care of our Time'. Taylor, as a priest of the Caroline church, was in effect the representative of a prohibited and persecuted form of religion, but he speaks in language which might be that of any sober Puritan: 'For we must remember that we have a great work to do, many enemies to conquer, many evils to prevent, much danger to run through, many difficulties to be mastered, many necessities to serve, and much good to do, many children to provide for, or many friends to support, or many poor to relieve, or many diseases to cure, besides the needs of nature and of relation, our private and our public cares, and duties of the world, which necessity and the providence of God hath adopted into the family of religion.'

The 'Twenty-three Rules for employing our Time' contain much that would recommend itself to any tradesman or farmer: 'Let every man that hath a calling, be *diligent* in the pursuit of its employments, so as not lightly or without reasonable occasion to neglect it in any of those times which are usually and by the custom of prudent persons and good husbands, employed in it.' 'It is better to plough upon holy days than to do nothing.' 'Let all persons of *all conditions* avoid delicacy and niceness in their *clothing* or *diet*, because such softness engages them upon great mis-spendings of their time...' The second chapter, 'Of Christian Sobriety', is no less near the bone: 'Accustom thyself to cut off all superfluity in the provisions of thy life; for our desires will enlarge beyond the present possession so long as all the things of this world are unsatisfying.' 'A temperate man is not curious of fancies and deliciousness. He thinks not much, and speaks not often, of meat and drink.' 'He that is proud of riches is a fool.' 'If a man be exalted by reason of any excellence in his soul, he may please to remember that all souls are equal.' The chapter 'Of Christian Justice' begins with 'Obedience to our Superiors', not the first thing that comes to mind with most purveyors of Christian opinion, in these days, when they hear the word 'justice'. 'That part of justice which is due from Superiors to Inferiors' comes next. Then contracts: 'Religiously keep all promises and covenants, though made to your disadvantage, though afterwards you perceive you might have done better.' Then restitution. The chapter is addressed to the individual conscience, seen in relation to a man's own actions and to matters within his power; the contemporary vulgarity, from which prominent churchmen are far from free, of seeing 'justice' in terms of what other men, and other people's governments, ought to be doing, is not even thought of; let a man search his own conscience, Taylor would have said.

If the disarray of the English church from 1645 to 1660 accounts for Taylor's retreat from public life and his preoccupation with the relatively eirenic questions of private conduct, it was a conscientious disqualification for office in the restored church which sent William Law (1686-1761) in a similar direction. Law was a brilliant controversialist, as the *Three Letters to the Bishop of Bangor* show. But though caught by his scruples in the toils of the Non-Juring movement, he came too late to contribute to its more public phase. He was moreover of a quietist temperament, as shown in the *Serious Call to a Devout and Holy Life* (1729), and he was even more concerned than Taylor with 'Showing how great devotion, fills our lives with the greatest peace and happiness that can be enjoyed in this life.' One is conscious of the existence of an extensive middle class with time on their hands. There is, anyhow, a certain lack of robustness about the Non-Jurors, as of men who enjoyed their consciences in quiet rather than face the ordinary rumbustious world. This is the case with Thomas Ken (1637-1711), in the first generation of what threatened in time to become a sort of ecclesiastical club, frequented by men of scholarly tastes, and surely Edward Stillingfleet (1635-99) was right to argue against his position, that a political schism was not free from blame and that Christians in the first centuries prayed for whatever emperor providence might send them. Law, however, though disqualified for ecclesiastical office, seems to have communicated in his parish church without scruple, and his writings show him, for all his quietism, to have a vivid sense of social appearances. Living contrary to the spirit of the world – the spirit which pursues wealth, fine houses, dignity, power, greedy or delicate eating or drinking – is what the book teaches: 'The history of the Gospel, is chiefly the history of Christ's *conquest* over this spirit of the world.' Devotion for him 'implies not any *form of Prayer,* but a certain form of life, that is offered to God not at any particular *times,* or *places,* but everywhere and in everything.' A man whose intention is to please God, can be 'a saint in his *shop*; his everyday business will be a course of wise and reasonable actions, made holy to God, by being done in obedience to his will and pleasure.' Once again, as with Jeremy Taylor, it is the world of the ordinary Christian which is in view, demanding though his notion of 'the Christian' is. It is for this reason, as well as because of Law's easy and pleasing style, that the *Serious Call* became and long remained one of the most popular of religious books, and for the same reason it should be read by all literate Anglicans now.

The tension between the world of conduct and the world of theology, between *mere* good conduct, which for the Christian includes prayer, and *mere* theology, is an irreducible part of institutional Christianity. Theological refinements, once outside the control of authoritarian government, whether ecclesiastical or lay, tend to divide; mere neighbourliness, as all history shows, tends not to succeed. No solution is attainable in this world, in spite of all the talk of ecumenicism. The shadow of politics cannot be removed from religion, for it is an essential element in religious and in other organization. The question is only how the shadow is to fall, and one may wonder how the prospects for the future are improved by aspirations towards administrative unity.

# Richard Baxter *

RICHARD BAXTER wrote a lot of books; 'very sad ones', Swift said, in a marginal note in Burnet's *History of my own Times* (1724-34). Burnet had computed the number of Baxter's books at 'near 200'; Baxter himself admitted to 128; there was much besides these volumes, including 'more Prefaces to the Works of others, than any Man of his time' had blessed the world with. N. H. Keeble, who has probably by now read as much of this author as anybody, concludes that 'even a sober judgment might claim not only that Baxter was the most voluminous theological writer in the English language, but that there can have been very few people who have ever written more in English than he'. That is something for *The Guinness Book of Records* but it does not in itself promise great happiness to the reader. One might ask, as with other records, whether such perseverance was really necessary.

Dr Keeble does not go so far as to assert that it was, but he gives us Baxter's apologia: 'Truly I have no Excuse or Argument but those of the Times, *Necessity and Providence.*' This of course had a suitable scriptural basis (1 Cor 9: 16), but the necessity laid upon Baxter 'to preach the gospel' hardly proves that he *had* to write 128 or 200 books; there might have been other ways of preaching, less tedious to posterity? To Baxter's credit, posterity was not what he was thinking about. He was concerned, like other practical men, with what seemed to him the needs of the moment; his accounting for his many books by the 'sudden occasions' that 'made them seem necessary at the time' suggests a sort of pious journalism. The ordinary comedy

* N. H. Keeble, *Richard Baxter: Puritan Man of Letters* (Clarendon Press)

of authorship is not far away, when we find him complaining that 'every ignorant, empty braine (which usually hath the highest esteem of its selfe) hath the liberty of the Presse', and his critics a few years later sneering at the 'multitudes of books, which he *voides* continually', or saying, as Bramhall did, that 'Mr Baxter's happiness is, only by turning the cock to spout out whole pages in an instant'.

Whether or not the proliferation of Baxter's books is attributable to a divine necessity, there was certainly a market for them. Keeble points out that 'religious publications comprise nearly half the total of all books published in England at least until 1640' and they formed a large part of publishers' lists for long after that. Moreover, for most of the seventeenth century discourse about politics tended to take the form of discourse about religion, and indeed the affairs of the day were religious affairs, whatever other elements they comported.

Baxter was the son of a yeoman, a Shropshire lad of the most authentic kind, and he had a largely country education, not finished off at a university; he carried this native milieu around with him, rather prominently, till the end of his days. He is 'an elusive figure', as Keeble says, but only in the sense that he cannot be pinned down, that he does not fit readily into any of the main categories in terms of which we are accustomed to think of the controversial history of the seventeenth century. As a person, he is not so much elusive as invincible, solid, pious, homely, peaceable, stubborn – a large, sensible man who was a pain in the neck to many but a vaguely reassuring presence to more, wherever he went, and reassuring because in a manner he was vague, in spite of all his attention to details. Towards the end of his life he attained a beautiful complacency, having learned, after emitting so many millions of words in preaching, counsel and in writing, that men are 'loth to be drenched with the truth', which was of course what he had always offered them. He had learned that 'in controversies it is fierce opposition which is the bellows to kindle a resisting zeal', so he became apt, he claims, to keep his judgment to himself: 'never', he says, 'to mention anything wherein I differ from another, or anything which I think I know more than he; or at least, if he receive it not presently, to silence it, and leave him to his own opinion'. He had become like some wise old general secretary of a trade union, of the old school, who has had his battles in his time and is capable of more, but would rather leave fools to talk, and get on quietly with the job.

But what was the job, as Baxter saw it? He lived from 1615 to 1691, and so on the inside of the seventeenth century, and if 'necessity' is a strong word to use by way of apology for all his voluminous discourses, what he saw as the needs of those around him certainly determined the main course of his life, as far as he could himself direct it. There is something profoundly characteristic about what he tells us of his domestic arrangements, which his wife ordered with 'so great skill and decency':

> I had been bred among plain, mean people, and I thought that so much washing of Stairs and Rooms, to keep them as clean as their Trenchers and Dishes, and so much ado about cleanliness and trifles, was a sinful curiosity, and expence of servants time, who might that while have been reading some good Book. But she that was otherwise bred, has somewhat other thoughts.

No doubt it would have been better if the servants had been reading *The Saint's Everlasting Rest* instead of scrubbing floors, and no doubt Baxter was too well looked after to know much about such things. There is indeed, about the immense theological discursiveness of the seventeenth century, more than a suggestion of sober entertainment, of filling in vast tracts of time which would otherwise have been empty. There was after all no television, and respectable people did not go to ale-houses or join in the sports of what Baxter, as freely as any college-bred divine, called 'the rabble'. He was every inch a man of the godly middle sort, moderate in respect of everything except his passion for writing. Not a man of wild prophecies or sudden conversions, he was above all social and conciliatory, and wanted to go to heaven in as numerous a company as might be. He had a 'public mind'; thought much of 'the excellency and necessity of self-denial' and of 'loving our neighbour as ourselves', and hated 'the radical, universal, odious sin of selfishness'. He was at least as much concerned with the well-being of the commonwealth as with his own sanctity.

With such concerns, he worked out a conception of Christianity which was suited to those 'divers obscure persons, not noted for any extraordinary profession, or forwardness in religion, but only to live a quiet, blameless life'. Such people will live under any institutional form, it may be under any religion, and perhaps Philemon and Baucis are as near the mark as the unobtrusive members of English congregations. But for Baxter, in his place and time, what they seemed to need was a religion of 'The Creed, the Lord's Prayer, the Ten Commandments', and he came to feel that he 'had rather read or hear of them, than of any of the school niceties, which once so pleased' him.

And, for all his reflections about speaking Turkish and going to convert the Turks, it was the Church of England, if there could be such a thing, which seemed to him the centre of the commonwealth. This meant for him all the Christians in the kingdom, united in the merest Christianity or in what they could swallow. 'It is nothing but a Christian Kingdom consisting of a Christian supreme Power, and combined Christians as Churches governed by that Power.' As to Papists, it was not their 'errors in the doctrines of faith' that 'were their most dangerous mistakes'; the 'great and unreconcileable differences' lay 'in their Church tyranny and usurpations' – a point of view worth thinking about, though apparently little in the mind of the masters of the present incomprehensive Church of England. Baxter laid it down that 'all coercive power about religion', the settling of the privileges of the several churches, and keeping the peace between them, should be a matter for the ordinary government of the country, which he was still able to think of as 'all Christian princes and governors'.

Baxter, so full of good ideas and of the will to conciliate in particular situations, did not perform with great distinction at the Savoy Conference which settled the Prayer Book of 1662, though the same might be said of other participants, on both sides. Busy as ever, and one might say full of his own fleas, he arrived with his own version, naturally of enormous length, the 'Confession of Sin', said not by the people but for them by the minister, who no doubt could say it better, being three and a half pages. Even with a more conciliatory bench of bishops, this would hardly have been the way to make progress. (The idea of an *Alternative Service Book,* with something for – nearly – every taste, had not yet been thought of.) An admittedly unsympathetic historian, Jeremy Collier (1650-1726), says of Baxter at the Conference: 'His talent lay in retiring to foreign distinctions, and misapplications of the rules of logic. But whether this involving the argument, and raising a mist, was art, or infirmity, is hard to determine.' However that might be, Baxter's view, as summarized by Keeble, was that 'by the will of God, the Savoy Conference failed: but to mortal eyes the prejudice and policy of the bishops ensured its failure'.

Baxter was convinced that he spoke for 'the greatest number of the godly' in England; in a sense he did, and not least in their muddles, their moderation, their pigheadedness, their dislike of ecclesiastical fripperies and theological refinements. Whether so much good sense is compatible either with full orthodoxy or with radical innovation, may be doubted, but it would be tolerant of both. It is, really, a political virtue, the essential virtue of a modern democracy, in which complacency has its part. It is perfect within established orders, and Baxter himself would have lived peaceably in any order that was incontrovertibly established. In the division of his times, he was thrown back on this notion of 'the greatest number of the godly', which in the real world raises questions as to who are the godly, and whether the greatest number of them are so godly as to be right. This makes problems of church order almost insoluble.

Keeble sums up Baxter's attitude by saying that he 'did not

choose between rival positions because he "could not" but because he "would not" ', which is convincing until one asks whether we can choose to be otherwise than we are. Anyhow the words indicate the diversity of Baxter's approaches to the problems of his day, and a 'rejection of partisanship' which is supposed to be more the temper of our own times than it was of his. What emerges from this study of him as a man of letters is not a writer who can be recommended, as such, to any but the most pertinacious, but a patient and practical man whose patience and practicality demanded a great deal of the same qualities in other people. Baxter was, after all, a man of more words than it takes to convince those who are willing to be convinced, and the others, as he came to see for himself, never will be. If this is the 'Puritan man of letters', as indeed it is, then, worthy though the model was, we need some other. 'To omit one warning, argument, reason, incentive, or illustration, or to neglect to counter a single error, temptation, or misunderstanding' was, for Baxter, as Keeble puts it, 'to run too grave a risk of failing the reader on the very point where he might need guidance'. The risk for such a writer is that the reader might fail him, as has happened to Baxter: 'Perhaps you may think I Digress from the matter in hand: But as long as I speak but for my Lord Christ, and for *Doing Good,* I cannot think I am quite out of my way.' But these are large claims, and Good is a dangerous thing to be sure you are Doing. Moreover, good writing has its own necessity, a humble one no doubt, but even a divine should think carefully before he asserts that he is excused from it.

# A Viewpoint on the Book of Common Prayer

ONE of the ugliest things about the row which has been set off by the recent petition in favour of the Authorized Version and the Prayer Book is the blind fury, in certain quarters, at the mere notion that 600 laymen chosen as 'representing aspects of national life, more especially in the arts', should venture to meddle in matters which, these critics said, were no business of theirs. The signatories might be musicians, sculptors, actors, scholars in various disciplines including literature and theology, they might be novelists, soldiers, they might – to sink to the lowest point in the scale of things – even be *poets*. What had the language of the Bible and Prayer Book to do with them? These books, to which generations of English speakers have owed an essential part of their education, were the private property, it was implied, of the bishops and clergy and of those laymen whom a very peculiar series of elections had brought to membership of that patently unsatisfactory body, the Synod of the Church of England.

That there should be a widespread concern for the beauty and homeliness of the Authorized Version was itself an offence. Beauty is the sign of the devil's work! That cry has been heard before. The Bishop of Peterborough, a distinguished witness and apparently one of the few bishops moved by this assault on our heritage, said in a letter to *The Times* (19 November 1979): 'One or two of the speeches in the recent Session of Synod might have come from the lost and unspeakable speeches of Attila the Hun.'

It is not the intention of the bishops and clergy who are mainly responsible for the state of affairs to which the Church of England has been brought to *burn* the offending books. The intention is merely that they should grow dusty in corners, or stay locked in vestries, while their place on the lectern and in the pews is taken by the lucubrations of – as David Martin has said – mid-Atlantic linguistic bureaucracies and their offshoots. Anyone who takes the trouble to look into half-a-dozen churches and inspect the books can confirm this – if he has not already been painfully alerted by what is going on in his own parish.

The methods by which these changes have been brought about have not always been above suspicion, and the Synod itself can hardly be said to have won its way into the hearts of ordinary churchgoers, who in general have been utterly unaware of what they were up to. These questions of Church government have their own importance, not only in what the bishops might regard as the proper places but for all who care for the openness and integrity of our national institutions; but it is the wider implications of what is going on that I wish to consider here.

Can it really be said that the language of the Church is of no concern to anyone but her officials? Such a claim – which is implicit in so much that has been said about the petition – is in reality so monstrous as to be full of the direst consequences for the Church itself. For there are many who are not Christians – people who understandably find that all their patience and intelligence in other fields of inquiry, and even the excursions they have made into the theology of the day, do not bring them to the point of entertaining the kind of belief which is required for even a half-acceptance of the traditional doctrines – who none the less admit the right of others to such belief and would wish to keep open the channels of communication with their Christian contemporaries and – as everyone who understands the point of liberal studies at all must do – with the past.

The impoverishment of the life of the nation, which depends on its *intellectual* life to a degree which the philistines are always unwilling to admit, must be enormous if these channels are not kept open. The fate of the Church – humanly speaking – could in these circumstances only be one of increasing degradation.

It must decline into a foolish sect, unable in the end to talk to the simplest intelligence because it has turned aside from its task of convincing the most able or even as much as impinging on their concerns. For a contrary view, one might turn to Augustine or Dante, but what is that to a Church which turns its back on Hooker and Berkeley and Butler?

Of course there are arguments for the use in church of a language 'understanded of the people', but the crass ignorance of many of the apologists of the New English Bible and the Good News Bible and the services known as 'Series 3' is that they suppose that such speech is within the grasp of anyone who chooses to open his mouth, and certainly of the respectable scholars and public relations men who have put the current inferior wares on the market. Of course, to be 'understanded of the people' on any subject is a matter of the greatest difficulty, and on matters so little in the ordinary course of listening and viewing as the Incarnation and its consequences there may perhaps be a little more than the common difficulty.

This is a problem which those who have a cure of souls have always to reckon with, when they are not deflected into the easier task of delivering moral discourses which would sound well at the United Nations. It is perhaps less the lack of receptivity in the congregations – which is no novelty – than an understandable feeling of ineptitude on the part of the clergy, which makes so many of them crave a Bible and liturgy which is not in that funny old language – as it seems to the less literate among them. Here one enters upon a field in which it is insulting for a layman even to open his mouth. But at the risk of being misconstrued, one may say that the clergy will not escape their duty of exposition by degrading the quality of the subject of their exposition. No one is seeking to discourage them from using all the resources of contemporary thought and speech in their sermons or in their discourses with the faithful and the unfaithful. On the contrary, it is precisely those menacing outsiders – less full of malice than seems to be supposed – who *want* such discourse to reach the level of general intelligibility it must reach if there is to be any possibility of a future society with some tincture of Christianity.

So great was the indignation of those who condemned the petition because 'some atheists signed with great fervour, holding that it was a national question', that they gave no weight to the fact that the signatories who might fall within that description were appearing side by side with men in Holy Orders, though for fear of embarrassing them 'very few clergymen were approached', and that the body of petitioners included a great many, perhaps a majority, who were familiar with the life of the Church, and very many who were communicants of more or less regularity. No conclusive statement can be made on this topic because the signatories were – properly, as it seems to many of us – simply not asked what their standing with the Church was. It is surely a bad day for the Church of England when it turns its back on the laity because they are not fully paid-up members. That is a point of view utterly sectarian and un-Anglican. 'What has the Church to do with the national heritage?' some clerics have asked, displaying an utter ignorance of what has been entrusted to them by their great forbears and proving that they have never considered the contents of that Prayer Book which they are busy shuffling out of sight. However, the matter will not be so easily resolved. There is too much life in the old book yet, as in the Authorized Version which will rise and smite them hip and thigh.

What do the furniture-removers suppose the Church of England will look like when they have finished their work? Do they suppose we go to church to listen to *them*? To hear the latest news from Synod? To hear what the World Council of Churches is up to in the way of amateur politics? Or that we shall choose the times of service to admire the buildings, like blundering tourists? Not at all. The Bible and the Prayer Book were what gave the services of the Church of England not only their splendour but their meaning, and some who came into the Church, not lightly and unadvisedly, but after mature reflection and through a desire for the sacraments, now feel so betrayed that the sacraments themselves cannot be taken in this desolation, for a moment must come when ignorance deprives us of their meaning and their mystery. I venture thus far beyond what might be thought the proper field of the *Times Literary Supplement* because it has been assumed by many apologists of the new versions that the question of language has nothing to do with the theological functions of the Church. It has. Those to whom these things mean nothing may still be scandalized that a national institution should see fit to declare, through the actions and inaction of its governing body, that literacy and integrity of speech have nothing to do with the concerns which concern them.

That no bishop – that the Archbishop of Canterbury himself – should not have risen in Synod to put in a good word for the volumes entrusted to him at his ordination, that none should have felt obliged, in the face of a petition signed by six hundred persons of good standing in the Commonwealth, to explain to the flock what value was now to be placed upon these treasures, is something so monstrous as to lead some of us to suppose that the Church of England has, in effect, resigned. She no longer speaks to the nation or even attempts to do so, for what has she to do with publicans and sinners, let alone artists who are the worst of the lot?

It is a blind retreat. But human beings will use the difficult art of speech, and a refusal to meet the petitioners on that ground exposes a profound evasion of all the issues, theological and political as well as linguistic, which gave and give life to the work of the great Anglican figures of the past. Is that all nothing? Then let the bishops reflect on what Coleridge said of our 'loved and prized' version of the Bible: 'Without this holdfast, our vitiated imaginations would refine away language to mere abstractions'. It is happening now. Let those – whether Christians or not – who have or teach children at least see that they get the Authorized Version.

# Poetry and Sincerity

MODERNITY has been going on for a long time. Not within living memory has there ever been a day when young writers were not coming up, with shining faces and a threat of iconoclasm, to destroy the illusions of their elders and the forms and rules into which they had hardened. Indeed such conduct has, for several generations at least, been so perfectly the tradition that most of the old now belong to it. It is *the* tradition, so far as the literature of the twentieth century is concerned, just as revolution, in some degree or other, has become the political tradition – the amount of novelty, in both cases, being much exaggerated by the patter that goes with it.

The theory of modernity propounded by Donald Wesling in *The Chances of Rhyme* * is that there are a lot of rules of rhyme and prosody – all pretty well bashed by now, one would think – and that to be modern is to bash still harder, yet to find, miracle of miracles, that the structure never entirely disintegrates. What is the hammer which is used in this vain effort at destruction? It is 'sincerity' – that venerable *pons asinorum* – so that the whole thing boils down to what was neatly put by Herbert Read, more than fifty years ago, as follows:

> The modern poet does not deny the right of regular verse to exist, or to be poetic. He merely affirms that poetry is sincerity, and has no essential alliance with regular schemes of any sort. He reserves the right to adapt his rhythm to his mood, to modulate his metre as he progresses.

* Donald Wesling, *The Chances of Rhyme: Device and Modernity* (University of California Press)

37

For 'poetry is sincerity' Professor Wesling reads 'everything in the poem, even the prosody, bears the mark of the poet's personality'. These are not easy conceptions. Nor does one get out of the difficulties by asserting, with Philip Larkin – in unfamiliar guise as a metaphysician – that 'every poem must be its own freshly created universe'.

W. P. Ker said soberly, some seventy years ago:

> When you talk about the form of a poem, what do you mean? We talk of the form of a poem, we talk of its matter: it may be assumed that in this case as in others the two terms are correlative.
>
> But as soon as one begins to examine into the meaning of the terms, they not only elude you, but they even exchange their meanings.

For the poet actually writing a poem these categories simply do not exist at all. The first necessity is to have something to say, but even this will be present only as an impending cloud, and to assert its necessity is to make an *ex post facto* analysis. The moment announces itself by words conveying a rhythm or, it may be, by a rhythm conveying a few words. There must be poets – Roy Fuller or the Poet Laureate – who take a solemn decision at some stage that there shall be *x* syllables to a line and a rhyme-scheme *abab* or whatever it is. I suspect that, in the heyday of, say, the sonnet, it was rather that the rhythms and rhymes so presented themselves, the language being at a stage in which that form was the natural vehicle for minds heavy with a certain class of utterance. For Sidney to 'look in his heart and write' was to write a sonnet; this form, then so little exploited in England, offering a way so clear that it was *the* way to say what he had to say. For the Elizabethan and Jacobean dramatists, some variant of the iambic pentameter was the indisputable language of the stage, so that the discourse came in that form till Shakespeare tore the medium to pieces and there seemed to be no more to be said in that way. The makers of the ballads must be supposed not to have hesitated over the form they should use. For the contemporary writer, no such resolute direction presents itself. Yet the problem remains the same: How is the poet to disburden himself of his thoughts with conviction?

The history of versification is really nothing else than the history of how such utterance has been possible, and there is more of necessity than of freedom in it, unless one can talk of a freedom to avoid the unnecessary. The conception Wesling appears to have, of 'art sentences' supported by all manner of rhetorical devices, so that the writer 'separates his language from ordinary language by a conscious patterning' is surely utterly wrong-headed, the product of a critical decadence which is suffering from too many books, too much leisure, too much discourse accompanying a shrivelled performance. Only the rhetorician, not of a silver age but of an age of tin or plastic, could ask 'what devices a work employs to achieve a relative transparence, or seeming spontaneity of rhetoric'. Such a question is surely designed to mislead both reader and writer as to the nature of its alleged subject-matter. It is calculated to increase the already overwhelming number of transgressions in verse by people nature never intended for poets. No less sinister is the spurious contrast between 'literary dialect' and 'the vernacular' and between 'literary poetry and inferior or non-literary poetry'.

Such an emphasis on the wilful elements in verse reflects a critical milieu in which too much is made of the separateness of 'poetry' from ordinary speech on the one hand and from good workmanlike prose on the other. The root of language is that vulgar *eloquentia* of which Dante wrote, and which he distinguished from the secondary speech 'which the Romans called grammar' in which we can be 'guided and instructed' only by 'the expenditure of much time, and by assiduous study'. 'Of these two kinds of speech', as Dante says, 'the vernacular is the nobler... necessary for all... even women and children.' (It is universality Dante is seeking to indicate by this last, now offensive, phrase.) The nursery rhyme is so far from being something to be dismissed with 'failed poetry' and other 'sub-literary genres' that it is the original and most important element in poetic education. Lose that – as it is being lost – and an essential tie with the language we learned 'by imitating our nurses', as Dante says, is gone:

> Gay go up and gay go down
> To ring the bells of London Town

> or

> Hink, spink, the puddings stink,
> The fat begins to fry,
> Nobody at home but jumping Joan,
> Father, mother and I.

Without such things it is not conceivable that Shakespeare would have written – if he did not rather heave out of memory, with more or less variation:

> Jog on, jog on, the footpath way,
> And merrily hent the stile-a;
> A merry heart goes all the day,
> Your sad tires in a mile-a.

'Poetry takes on a life beyond techniques', says Wesling, meaning that this happens after 1795 – his date for the beginning of Romanticism and so of modernism – and that thereafter rhymes and all his array of other devices are suspect. This timing is historically myopic. Poetry as the thing to be said, the thought to be disburdened, has *always* taken priority over the abstractions of 'technique'. Nursery rhymes actually *say* things; even the counting-out of a game rhyme is a meaning to be conveyed – and one of great seriousness.

To maintain the relationship of verse with workmanlike prose is a need not less frequently ignored. Because the writing of 'poetry' is encouraged on a doctrine of self-expression – a luxury-derivative from that religion of democracy which has so largely replaced Christianity – there is a sort of vulgarization of creation, of the kind adumbrated by Philip Larkin. Thousands who could not write a straight sentence of prose to convey some ordinary matter of fact, are encouraged to believe that they are engaged in a superior activity because their lines do not quite reach the margin and are therefore called verse.

It might be too much to say that no one who cannot write prose should be allowed to write verse, but certainly no one should be admitted to any of those myriad courses which purport to teach the writing of verse, until he has read at least one book each of Swift and Defoe and can write a page which is not too utterly disgraceful by their standards.

Poetry – verse in any serious usage of the term – is a receptacle for sense which cannot be put into prose, and which burdens the speaker until it is said. 'Lully, lulla, thou little tiny child' is a paradigm of the art; the assonance and half rhyme, and the rhythm, are rigorously essential to the meaning to be unloaded. The line says what cannot be said otherwise. Poetry is precisely that; all other speech hangs more or less loosely. Only the greatest poets maintain this degree of rigour at any length.

We live amidst such a plethora of bad verse, in an age of such disastrous facility of speech and writing of all kinds, that the very notion of the rarity of humanly indispensable utterance is on the way to being lost. Real speech has to be surrounded by silence. We get this impression – in part, admittedly, because of what has been lost – in the fragments which remain to us of early literatures – from our own Anglo-Saxon, for example. What is certainly not illusory is the growing facility, over the centuries, in the use of specific forms. We see the author of *Gawain* introducing variants to avoid the facility into which Langland is already falling. I regret not having made more use of the opportunities I once had for learning Anglo-Saxon and Middle English, and speak very tentatively on these matters, but I suppose that the relative slackness of Langland's verse represents the growing unsuitability, for the language of the fourteenth century, of a form of parallelism which was the product of a stronger, inflected, language.

Chaucer's triumphant solution of the problem was the adaptation of French versification and rhyme-schemes, so far as but no farther than the language allowed. This adaptation must have been felt as a release, not as the entry into new trammels. It brought a new clarity into English verse; the language itself grew clearer:

> Hyd, Absolon, thy gilte tresses clere;
> Ester, ley thou thye mekness al a-doun;
> Hyd, Ionathas, al thy friendly manere;
> Penalopee, and Marcia Catoun,
> Mak of your wyfhod no comparisoun;
> Hyde ye your beautes...

– and so on. It is a measure of the genius of Chaucer that he could perceive and realize these new possibilities of the language throughout the eight thousand lines or so of *Troilus and Criseyde*. His contemporary, John Gower, is fumbling by comparison, or at any rate mechanical. Gower's French poems are better than his English poems and that was no doubt because there was more in his aural memory to help him in French.

The balance between the degree of memory which indicates a direction of movement, and a degree of emancipation from it which enables the words to come freshly, is what determines the rise and fall of particular verse forms. The work of Chaucer determined without appeal the direction of the future development of English verse, but it is rarely that one feels that his immediate successors are as at home as he was with the new demands, while the old way had fallen into a measure of old-fashionedness which made it unusable. There are those in whom a residual alliteration remains; there are those in whom rhyme falls into a simple trot; there are – even up to Sackville, magnificent though he sometimes is – those who appear to find the structures they use somewhat unwieldy. Some of the best verse of the fifteenth and early sixteenth centuries is by men who were applying Chaucer's discoveries to a different variant of the language – Scots – without much in the way of technical novelty. The real infusion of easiness into a variety of rhymed forms in English must have come from popular poetry:

> I have a newe gardyn,
> & newe is be-gunne;
> swych an-other gardyn
> know I not under sunne,

or

> I must go walke the wood so wyld,
> & wander here & there.

Conflating the history, one may say that perfection in a new kind – a lesser achievement than Chaucer's but still an immense triumph of lucidity – came with Wyatt, who of course drew on the technical achievements of French and Italian. He may be said to have made these achievements truly at home by assimilating to his versions of them the singableness of popular verse. One knows how, a little later, Sidney still had an ear for the border ballads, and no doubt he was not alone in this. Perhaps it is not fair to take Charles d'Orléans, in spite of his long years in England, as an example of the difficulty of making a transfer of techniques from one language to another, but it is worth noting how his competent enough English verses fail altogether to show the life of his rondeaux and ballades in French.

Marks of a new confidence at once in the aural qualities of English verse and in its ability to convey whatever needs to be said, are everywhere in Elizabethan poetry. Something new appears with Gascoyne – whose merits are still hardly enough recognized – in the realistic ease with which he lays before us, when a prisoner in the Low Countries, his insistent worries about the fate of his gun. Not for nothing did this accomplished performer urge poets not to worry too much about technique but first to be sure that they really had something to say. In the move towards suppleness and lucidity, verse, at this epoch, leads prose by rather more than a short head, and it is this, no doubt, which gave confidence – sometimes excessive confidence – in the writing of long poems. The pressure to speak in ways prose cannot manage must always be the motive for verse, and there was still much that prose could not manage. It is in Spenser that the ability to speak at length without losing the thread either of aural or semantic satisfactions, first achieved a new suppleness. He demonstrated this suppleness through complicated stanzas and thousands of lines, and his occasional superficial archaisms will not distract anyone who reads him at length from the general urbanity of his language – an indispensable contribution to later developments.

The Elizabethan and Jacobean eras left English a mature language – that is to say one always threatened by the nibblings of decline. It seems odd if not ungrateful to talk of the varied achievements of the seventeenth century in this way, but they became varied by limiting themselves in one direction or another – as who could do otherwise, after Shakespeare? There are the refinements of the song-writers, often exquisite, but unable to go beyond Campion and Shakespeare; there are the specialist achievements of the Metaphysicals and related poets. There is Milton's personal form of elaboration. Above all – as regards significance for later times – there is the movement which took the heroic couplet from Ben Jonson to Dryden, with a variety of interesting manifestations on the way. With the possible exception of the song-writers – who however have a new tone to offer, identifiable only in their day – these were all ways of pushing the subject-matter of poetry in new directions. The couplet was perhaps the nearest thing to a deliberate aim at a new rhetoric, an attempt to look smarter than prose which was in fact overtaking verse as an expository medium. This is one of the few examples in the history of English verse of a development which put a lid on what the poet had to say rather than took it off; and here, a driving force was the sharper opportunities which the closed couplet gave to satire.

Until perfected. For when Pope had done all that could be done in the way of closing the couplet and regulating the caesura it was not long before the familiarity of the preferred pattern became too great to be borne. Whatever may be said for this or that later exponent of the form, it needed the full mind of Wordsworth to replace it decisively; he felt the need to do away with baubles and to speak as 'a man speaking to men'. At this point, Wesling would say, a new world began, although others would say that there was the same motive for change that there had always been.

That is already nearly two hundred years ago. Wesling sees a new Romantic rocket shot from the first about 1910, and although he speaks boldly of 'many major poets' since that date, in any serious historical perspective it would be difficult to substantiate that description. It is hard to find much radical novelty in English verse (in which I include that written in America) after 1920, which is not to say that there are not to be found a few people who have been impelled by a hitherto unspoken content to invent new tones and occasional new rhythms. To liberate the language, even ever so little, from the shadow of what has become familiar, and walk a few paces on firm ground, is still the business of the poet, as it always was. A language so worn by use as ours is may give the illusion that anything can be said in it, but the difficulties are certainly not less than they were, and may well be greater. Professor Wesling tells us that Miss Wesling, a poet aged seven, speaks 'as an individual'. She should place a steadying hand on her father's arm and suggest that he looks up her sources.

# The Alternative Service Book *

IT has long seemed to me that the Book of Common Prayer could do with a little editing. The exhortations, which are never used, in the Communion service might perhaps be relegated to an appendix; there might be some clearer indication of the date of Easter, than the Table to find Easter Day; the Golden Numbers - but no, surely they must be supposed to have charm, in a world which prides itself on its numeracy. Very little would be needed to make the book easier for congregations to handle: for that matter, they have managed to handle it for upwards of three or four hundred years. However, the ecclesiastical authorities have now given us something better - or at any rate bigger. Here, in some thirteen hundred pages, is the result of a labour which has occupied 'first the Convocations and the House of Laity, and latterly the General Synod, for more than fifteen years'. It is with relief that one learns that this publication marks a pause in their 'programme of liturgical business'.

The book looks more like the product of a programme of liturgical business than the kind of simplification one might have hoped for. It is true that the date of Easter, up to the year 2025, can now be determined by a glance at a new table; there is a Table of Transference to amuse learned children during the sermon, and it is simpler than the Prayer Book exercise with Golden Numbers. But the pattern of the services themselves is of bewildering complexity. This book makes too modest a claim, when it calls itself the Alternative Service

* *Alternative Service Book 1980* (CUP/Clowes/SPCK;
OUP/Mowbrays/Hodder and Stoughton editions with and
without Psalter)

Book. It is no mere alternative to the Book of Common Prayer, but contains within itself so many varied forms of service that it would be better called the Book of Alternatives. One gathers that those fifteen years of liturgical business did not end in anything that could be called unanimity, unless an exhausted agreement to differ can be called that. It is not that the ancient theological controversies are not muted. They are, although their aged heads pop up here and there. But what the variety of services primarily represents is a variety of tastes; there is certainly no objective principle which could determine the choice of one set of services rather than another. There are alternative blessings and alternative confessions. A bit of what you like does you good - that seems to be the underlying principle: what you like - within limits.

'Unity need no longer be seen to entail strict uniformity of practice', says the Preface. It can hardly be said that *strict* uniformity has been seen within living memory, and indeed the long years of indiscipline among the clergy are an important part of the background to the present disintegrative book. What is new now is that the notion of a standard of practice has in effect been abolished. So we have 'The Order for Holy Communion Rite A' and 'The Order for Holy Communion Rite B', but each of these proves, on examination, to offer a number of variants, to be adopted or not according to the devices and desires of clergy or congregations, or whoever is strong enough among them to get his way. Do you prefer the first, second, third or fourth eucharistic prayer? The first or the second intercession? And so on. Variety is the spice of life, they say; it is less certain that it should spice liturgy to the extent that no one but an expert in Alternative Services can really keep up with it, and that going into a church beyond his own parish boundary no one will know what he is going to find. Indeed, he will be lucky if he knows what he will find in his own parish.

All this is supposed to be good. It has, however, until recently been a predominant part of Christian education for the churchgoer to hear familiar words until he knows many of them by heart. Not for me to say what may happen to souls, under the old dispensation or the new, but under the old, *minds* were actually filled with something. Not only were the words of Matins and Evensong, the Communion service, and the psalter, so familiar as to be only just below the surface in the memories of ordinary Anglicans; the system provided for the public reading of the Bible in the Authorized Version. This education has, admittedly, long been slipping with the decline in churchgoing and the virtual elimination – by the authorities – of Matins and Evensong as popular services; but the slipping cannot be taken as an argument for letting it slide altogether. The fruit of excessive variety will certainly be even greater ignorance, for let no one suppose that people will possess anything of the wealth of the Christian tradition unless they learn something first. Even the Lord's Prayer is now on sale in three versions – that of the Book of Common Prayer, which until recently every decently brought up child knew; that of Rite A *et passim* and that of Rite B *et passim*. The latter varies from the true English version only by tiny verbal changes so silly that no one but a pedant could have thought of making them at all – changes which, moreover, no one familiar with any range of English as it is spoken today could imagine would be clearer to anybody. So many people must have had a good idea during those laborious fifteen years, and so many people must have preferred their own good ideas to other people's, that there was no way of getting that much-to-be-desired pause in liturgical business except by concluding how right almost everybody was, and making a puzzle book of 1,300 pages.

The width of nefarious agreement over the text of the Alternative Book has been made possible by the fact that the book itself was strictly unnecessary. There was no great theological issue at stake, no anxiety widely and deeply felt which the book in any manner resolved. The difference from the situation in Cranmer's day, which is often invoked as a precedent and excuse, could not have been greater. Cranmer's books represented the resolution of agonizing differences; it is the lack of any comparable predicament at the origin of the new book which makes the latter so frivolous by comparison. Even the Prayer Book as proposed in 1928 was *about* something. Of course the Alternative Book has behind it the Continental liturgical movement and the stream of domestic scholarship for which Gregory Dix's *The Shape of the Liturgy* may stand as an indicator. Dix's bitter pages against Cranmer have had their influence here, as well as those more illuminating parts of his work which have a bearing on the changes in the order of the liturgy now ambiguously promulgated. But, important as these scholarly developments are, they represent a shallow stream compared with the discontents which burst upon Europe in the Reformation. It is the chance confluence of this stream with the real current of the age – a self-assertive humanism the history of which runs from the more extreme Protestantism of the Reformation, through Locke and Voltaire to the current religion of democracy – which has swept the present book into being. To that extent the authors of the Preface are certainly right when they say that 'those who seek to know the mind of the Church of England in the last quarter of the twentieth century will find it in this book'.

But what a mind! It is distressing to those who have known and loved the Church of England, not only in Cranmer but in Hooker, Herbert, Vaughan, Jeremy Taylor, Swift, Berkeley, Butler, Law and many another, to find to what mouthpieces she is now reduced. It is not those great men of the Anglican tradition who are the mere stylists; it is not even the signatories of David Martin's notorious petition who hanker after that distinction. The authors of the Alternative Service Book are the real literary gents. 'Composed in the very finest modern English', says the press release, 'this new service [*sic*] brings the form of Anglican worship right into the twentieth century.' Whoopee! In fact, there is hardly a page of straight twentieth-century prose in the whole volume. And as for the verses so coyly introduced into what used to be Evensong, they turn out to be by Robert Bridges: 'We see the evening light,/Our wonted hymn outpouring.' You need to be something of a stylist to see that as more in tune with the twentieth century than Bishop Ken.

The pretence of modernity is fundamental to the Alternative Book, and to apologias which have been so widely made for the new services. The practical thought in the mind of the more simple-minded parsons has been that there must be *some* reason why they could not keep their churches full, and that as everything really successful seemed to be *modern,* they had better try a bit of that themselves. That might not make church quite as acceptable as the telly, but they could try. The secret of many things, they had heard, was in good public relations. The Prayer Book and the Bible sounded so unfamiliar to those who were not familiar with them that it would be nice if things were said in such a way that everyone would think that they had heard them before, even though it was only because they had encountered just such language in the pages of the *Daily Telegraph* or some other 'quality' paper; so they started using translations of the Bible which sounded like that. (Only in limited circles is thinking yet advanced enough to look rather to the *Daily Mirror* as a model.)

Of course things did not work out exactly as had been hoped. One reason is that the ghosts of the Authorized Version and the Prayer Book were too powerful. It needs more than a prudential decision to speak of the things the Fathers of the sixteenth and seventeenth centuries spoke of, in a language which owes nothing to them. Echoes of the old speech sound through this new book, only the original rhythms have been nicked and chopped here and there and inept words introduced which do not carry conviction.

It may well be that the real difficulty about revising the Prayer Book at this time is that there is no contemporary theological language which really carries conviction. We have to have some patience in educating ourselves in our ancestors' language in order to know what they meant. I once heard a wretched child set up in church to read the story of the creation of Eve. The only comment one could make on the passage was that no one could believe a word of it. If such stories are not understood with the imagination they are not understood at all. The ordinary language of the twentieth century means by understanding something mainly mechanical and quantitative. Until this primary theological difficulty is faced, there can be no serious beginning of an attempt to restate the traditional matter of the Christian faith. And of course the restatement will be slow, partial, and hesitant – quite unlike the verse of Robert Bridges or the prose of Professor Frost.

It would seem all too simple a game to point to examples of sheer outrageous ineptitude in the language of the Alternative Book, were it not that many people including, it would seem, most of the bishops and a large majority of the other members of Synod, have their perception of language so blunted that they simply do not know the living word, and the living cadence, from the dead. This should not surprise us because the living has to be new and anyone familiar with literary history knows that, since the date of the *Lyrical Ballads* (1798) at the latest, it has taken several decades for any new tone to win public acceptance. That is a phenomenon of the current phase of the language from which the writers of liturgies have no celestial exemption. One might say that the project of an alternative book was doomed from the start, given the many hands that were to meddle with it and the representative approvals which had to be sought at all stages. These difficulties could have been foreseen, but only by people of more literary perspicuousness than, apparently, those who actually had charge of the Church's affairs. At the risk of encountering readers who cannot see what is wrong with the new versions, I will give a few items from a schedule of comparisons which might go on for ever.

Take Morning Prayer. One of the 'sentences' reads:

> In everything make your requests known to God in prayer and petition with thanksgiving. *Philippians* 4:6.

This is preferred to the Authorized Version's

> In everything by prayer and supplication with thanksgiving let your requests be made known to God.

Perhaps only a trained palate would observe the difference here, and markedly prefer the older version. It is also rather hard to see what constitutes the 'modernity' of the later version. Second item: as to rhythm, the Confession drags along like a lump of dead meat; but those who do not see that cannot be made to see it. More will recognize the effrontery of preferring a version of the *Venite* which has

> In his hand are the depths of the earth: and the peaks of the mountains are his also

in place of

> In his hand are all the corners of the earth; and the strength of the hills is his also.

The reader who cannot understand the enormity of the substitution is fit only to be a member of Synod. In the *Benedictus:*

> To shine on those who dwell in darkness and the shadow of death (ASB)

is not 'modern', but sham antique; and compare the rhythm with that of:

> To give light to them that sit in darkness, and in the shadow of death (BCP)

which is every whit as intelligible.

> Bless the Lord all created things: sing his praise and exalt him for ever. (ASB)

'Modern'? No, only mediocre sham religious. The earlier version, which is being pushed aside for this, is breath-taking:

> O all ye Works of the Lord, bless ye the Lord: praise him and magnify him for ever. (BCP)

As if in shame, the authors of the Alternative Book reprint the
Prayer Book versions of the Canticles in a sort of appendix to
Morning and Evening Prayer. If they had that much shame,
where was the courage which should have made them reject
the inferior versions altogether?

The case of the psalms is very odd indeed. The psalter did
not enjoy the benefit of 'repeated scrutiny by the General
Synod', but, desperate to have something worse than
Coverdale's (the BCP) version – as one easily might have – they
hit on the English text published in 1976 by David L. Frost,
John A. Emerton and Andrew A. Mackintosh. Good for them!
But bad for the rest of us and an irreparable loss to any
congregation that makes the changeover. 'Modern'? No. An
insensitive pastiche. There are some good laughs for the
student of the bogus contemporary.

> Praise him in the blast of the ram's horn:

sing our alternative Davids.

> Praise him in the sound of the trumpet:

answers old Coverdale from his tomb. Ah, Coverdale, we must
tell him; at least we moderns know it *was* a ram's horn, and do
not mix it up with any instrument we have actually heard in
the twentieth century.

One can only hope that when the Alternative Book at last
falls heavily into the pews, the eyes of priests and congregation
will be opened and they will see that this is not a Prayer Book
made new for the twentieth century but a compendium of old
hat including 500 pages of mutilated collects, sentences and
readings from every version of the Bible except the best. They
should laugh unsanctimoniously to see that the bishops have
promoted themselves above the Queen, in the Church of
England's first attempt since the Reformation to set itself apart
from the polity in which it lives; and to notice the concurrence
of innocent scholarship and political innuendo implied in the
odd name of 'President' given to the priest at Holy
Communion. I suggest that there should be a competition in

every parish for the most striking pair of comparative phrases from the old book and the new. When the congregation has played this game for a week or two, they should hunt round to see where the churchwardens have hidden their real Prayer Books, and blow the dust off them.

# The Company He Keeps *

IS IT a wise or a foolish man who, after more than seventy years in this hard world, comes before it as an optimist? The handsome head of John Redcliffe-Maud, alias Sir John Maud, GCB, CBE and what else, alias Baron of the City and County of Bristol, looks from the dust-cover with a questioning half-smile. In his Bath robes? Not a bath-robe, anyway, though it would need more than a head-and-shoulders portrait – or closer acquaintance with the official wear of knights and peers – to determine the question with precision. A handsome face, a noble bearing. A fine specimen, without a doubt, of the secondary public man of his epoch – of the race of heads of (the right) colleges, Permanent Secretaries, chairmen of Royal Commissions and the like, who live just below the surface of public events and pop up from time to time to give them momentarily an appearance of old-world respectability.

These are the men who soften blows and hold things together – or rather, they are the most eminent of them, for had the class not been a relatively large one, the process of disintegration would certainly have been more rapid and more painful than it has been. Lord Redcliffe-Maud possesses, in an outstanding degree, the qualities necessary for success in this field and his success has indeed been such as might well induce a certain optimism, even in a more cynical character. Cynicism is not one of Lord Redcliffe-Maud's strong points: it is indeed one for which one could not give him more than a gamma marking, as compared with other members of his class, but this defect has perhaps made him more rather than less

* John Redcliffe-Maud, *Experiences of an Optimist* (Hamilton)

suitable for public display. For Lord Redcliffe-Maud is, indubitably, a *nice* man, he would not hurt a fly or, if he did, it would be clear to everybody that it was for the best of motives.

Lest I should be thought to be claiming to draw a portrait from the live model, instead of merely giving an informed opinion, such as Lord Redcliffe-Maud has himself given on so many subjects, perhaps I should say that I set eyes on him only once. This was in 1950 when – as Permanent Secretary of the Ministry of Education – he gave an address on the beauties, and you might say the sacredness, of bureaucracy. He spoke less as a Permanent Secretary – they are a fairly hard-bitten race, in my experience – than as one of that dangerous class of persons, the Prominent Layman, and true to form told how bureaucrats could use their 'creative imaginations' to make a 'specifically Christian contribution' to what might seem to be the most dubious enterprises. I went on record at the time to suggest that there seemed to be some confusion between the Divine Will and the policy of His (then) Majesty's Government. Perhaps there was. Certainly reading *Experiences of an Optimist* has not entirely reassured me, but the revival of this memory of thirty years ago disposes of the possibility that the volume might be a product merely of the euphoria of old age.

Lord Redcliffe-Maud's own account of the book is that 'it is a volume of memoirs rather than autobiography', and he presents himself as 'the peg on which are hung the few bits of contemporary history' that he knew at first hand and 'can remember'. There are no indiscretions, public or private, for this is the man who, when taking part in BBC *Brains Trusts* never gave an answer which made trouble for himself or his Minister. A honeyed tongue! Before accepting a BBC invitation, he tells us, 'I always asked my Minister's advice. In fact none of my Ministers,' he goes on, 'whether man or woman, Socialist or Tory, wanted me to say no; they thought it useful that their chief adviser should sometimes expose himself as a human being whose mind and lips were not permanently sealed.' Especially useful, no doubt, because neither the lips nor the mind were too wide open, either. Maud was so much in the game that he seems to have been unaware – to be unaware even now – of his role as a man who would expose only the innocence of ministerial intentions and the high virtue of the milieu. From such a man one can expect no more than conventional portraits of those with whom his varied career brought him into contact. He is no Saint-Simon, even of the smallest size; he shows no sign of entering incisively into the motives of those he observes, any more than into his own. And since the 'few bits of contemporary history' he 'knew at first hand' are treated in so personal a vein, there is no hope of much enlightenment here as to their nature and consequences. The value of this book, such as it is, is rather as an account of a career, exemplifying brilliantly one type of operator – and that by no means the worst – in the last fifty years of public life in this country.

John Primatt Redcliffe-Maud was born in Bristol in 1906, the sixth and youngest child of the then vicar of St Mary Redcliffe, the great church in which Chatterton pretended to have discovered his forgeries, in the days before the arts had 'grown in popularity' and 'our creative artists' had 'transformed our reputation in the world', as the author tells has happened in his lifetime. From Summerfields, his first school, he won a scholarship to Eton, at the normal age of 13, after the 'appalling' disappointment of not having succeeded at the age of 12. At Eton 'revolutionary ideas' were in the air. 'Privilege of any kind was frowned upon.' (Not quite *any* kind, perhaps?) In the turn of time he was elected to Pop, that famous centre of egalitarianism for which the 'fount of honour' was the existing membership. In October 1924 he went up to Oxford, with a leaving scholarship from Eton and an open scholarship at New College. Something of the temper of his life as an undergraduate can be gathered from his comment that not all his 'Christian colleagues in the SCM can have thought acting in [the OUDS] Smoker something their President should do', and one ('only one,' he says rather oddly) 'lost his faith as a direct result of seeing' that great mans' performance. After four years of undergraduate life at Oxford, he had to think of a career. After a year at Harvard, he put himself into the hands of one of those London institutions 'long dedicated to coaching Civil Service candidates', where his new tutors, he says, shared his own pessimism about the outcome. This was not put to the test, for at the critical moment University College, Oxford had to find a junior research fellow who could act as dean, there being an absolute shortage of unmarried fellows living in college. Who more suitable than young Maud? The name had only to be mentioned to David Lindsay Keir and the job was done. Politics was to be his subject, it seems suddenly to have been decided. 'But why politics?' Why indeed? Anyhow, G.D.H. Cole put him on to the subject of local government; the Home University Library wanted a book on it and Maud's situation gave him the contract.

So began the working life of one who was to deplore ('now deeply,' he says in this book) the fact that all the friends of his boyhood went like himself to independent schools and that he 'grew up for 18 years knowing nothing of the great majority' of his contemporaries 'who went to maintained schools'. An optimist can find consolation everywhere, however, and while he went to Eton, Oxford and Harvard 'only because' he won scholarships, now he can look out on a world where '*every* boy and girl in Britain can go to a secondary school... and to a university – if they wish to go and are thought capable of staying the course'. Maud's pupils in politics included Stephen Spender – who does not seem to have learnt much politics anyway – and if it is not breath-taking, it does at least cause one to reflect on the insularity of the pre-war Oxford school of politics that it was only in 1938 that he 'spotted' the 'need for rearmament if Hitler and Mussolini were to be stopped'. He shared the enthusiasm of his father, by then Bishop of Kensington – an enthusiasm shared by how many more besides! – for 'what the League of Nations stood for', and seems to have regarded that as some sort of substitute for more substantial protection. He was in good company, and it is not too much to say that his genius, all his life, has been for being in good company rather than for actually being right. Perhaps those are harsh words, but certainly 1938 was a little late for news of Hitler to have reached one of the country's principal centres of instruction. Had he read *Mein Kampf?* Did he know anything about French politics? Not his subject, perhaps.

It was the war, anyhow, which finally launched Maud on his great career. By this time he was Master of Birkbeck College; it was William Beveridge, then Master of University College, Oxford, who contrived to get him to the Ministry of Food as a temporary principal, though admittedly no great contrivance was needed, in those days, to find a place in Whitehall for one who had the credentials of an Oxford don. For Maud this was the beginning of twenty years with 'delightful' and 'highly intelligent' people, among whom he was rapidly propelled to various senior positions in the Ministry of Food and the Reconstruction Office. The fact that his first assignment was in a 'general' division with wide and loosely-defined responsibilities, and not in one of the many concerned with the actual supply of meat, bacon or what-not, must have had something to do with this fast start; the fact that he was, as he says, 'ambitious' will have provided valuable motive power: but the determining factor was the favour of Lord Woolton. In 1945, when Maud became Permanent Secretary to the Ministry of Education, the immediate propellor was perhaps Morrison, whom he had met in Oxford and served in the Lord President's office. He had, in six years in the Civil Service, given ample evidence of his ability to survive. The world being what it is, and Whitehall being what it is, it cannot all have been done by 'a life that has a depth and breadth and quality which transcend dimensions either of time or space'. Maud was very much the sort of man the Civil Service wanted – by background and by temperament.

If he had a weakness, it must have been the delusion that he was doing good. Civil servants are, very properly, paid to do what has to be done, which is something different. One has some sympathy with those of Maud's colleagues who thought, he tells us, that the Arts Council took too much of his time, and

Unesco 'far too much', the more since there is nothing in this book to suggest that he had even a glimmering of foresight as to the political meaning of these organizations. Indeed, the overwhelming impression one gets is of a man who had no more sense of the direction in which society was changing than, as a teacher of politics before the war, he had had of the significance of Nazism. A certain discretion, in relation to the cant of the moment, is a prerequisite in a civil servant. Actually to believe it all, as Maud appears to have done, is surely going a bit far, however widely acceptable it may make one. The sense that there was never anything actually wrong about Maud's reactions, in the situations in which he found himself, is profoundly disquieting. Did he not sometimes think an unsuitable thought? Not even when George Tomlinson was, as he records, 'trying to persuade an official deputation from the Soviet Union who visited the Ministry' that the Ministry did not prescribe syllabuses. ' "No," said George, "we believe in making teachers earn their pay. What they teach is *their* business, not mine." ' George Tomlinson was a man of great charm, more likely to see the work of his department in terms of social comfort than of what used to be meant by education, and no doubt it was fortunate that he did not regard teaching as his business. Still, this little interview leaves many reverberations in the mind of the reader. How little, one cannot but reflect, it left in the mind of the author.

In 1952 Maud was moved to the Ministry of Power, an assignment perhaps less full of temptations for a man who was apt to indulge his taste for elevating tasks. Offered little opportunity for preachments by the subject-matter of his six years' work, Lord Redcliffe-Maud finishes his chapter with a piece of verbosity about 'openness and confidentiality in democratic government', 'realistic answers' and 'changing problems', in which no thought can be found. It must have been a problem for those concerned to know what to do with a man who had been promoted to Permanent Secretary at the age of 39, had behind him thirteen years in that rank, and was still some seven years from a date when he could decently be retired. So high marks go to whoever pushed him off to South Africa as High Commissioner and in due course Ambassador. The idea was perhaps suggested by his honeymoon visit to Africa more than a quarter of a century earlier. Moreover, here was a situation in which a high-minded man would look well. And so it was that when Harold Macmillan toured Africa in 1960 and made his famous wind of change speech, our man in Cape Town had a suitably incorruptible look. One phrase of Macmillan's speech is so in keeping with the tone of these memoirs that the reader may find himself attaching a certain significance to it in relation to the High Commissioner's biography: a 'society in which individual merit and individual merit alone is the criterion for a man's advancement whether political or economic'. Fine words! Summerfields, Eton, Oxford, Whitehall, with friends at every stage to help at the right moment: lucky, one may think, that this social ideal had not been realized in our own country when John Primatt was on his way.

What more suitable conclusion, to such a career, than the mastership of an Oxford college? Given the style in which the taxpayers of the world are accustomed to keep their diplomatic services – one supposes, in order to protect them from knowledge of the world – the Master's Lodgings at Univ. could be no more than an appropriate refuge. And indeed Lord Redcliffe-Maud is not ungrateful. He had come home and was well placed to know that 'headship of an Oxford college must have been, nearly always, one of the most enviable forms of life'. It is hard to imagine anyone better-equipped to fill such an office with grace, with all the little liberalisms and concessions to modern manners which the defence of such privilege now demands. The chapter devoted to the years 1963-76 is a recital of exercises in this tact, accompanied by a cooing over the improved intellectual standard of under-graduates and the accessibility of the pastures of Oxford to children from comprehensive schools. On this last delicate matter – as on how many encountered in his long career? – Lord Redcliffe-Maud admits 'we still have a long way to go'.

But the point about this incomparable operator is that he is always on the right course: 'we have made progress', and of course 'meanwhile, we could take more trouble to be fair'.

There is a chapter on 'Local Government, 1929-79' which recounts the progress of the young don who wrote the book for the Home University Library to the chairman of the Royal Commission. It would be unjust to hold Lord Redcliffe-Maud responsible for all the confusions that followed, for politicians competed hotly to make a mess of it, as is now generally recognized. One wonders, however, whether for once his tact did not desert him when he chose to elaborate his title by a reference to 'the City and County of Bristol', which now survives only in that title, and there only until this eminent public servant is gathered to whatever fields await such a man.

With what company? One cannot say, but that someone will already have put in a word for him must be as certain as anything in these grave matters. As regards himself, Maud's optimism in this world has been justified. What one finds harder to share is his optimism in relation to the world at large. 'Some things have hugely improved' since he was born, yes. But when one comes to some of his examples one cannot but feel that his euphoria should have been more tempered. 'Take education.' Well, take education. Or, 'I believe that Britain's greatness has actually increased.' Whatever may be meant by that dubious expression, has the progress been absolutely linear? 'We reached a new height of excellence in the art of government.' The art of *what?* Even (I quote) 'in collaboration with . . . the Soviet Union'. (Think nothing of those superficial troubles you sometimes read about in the papers.) 'I believe that the distinction we so often tend to make between the secular and the concern of Christians, between the pagan and the holy, is fundamentally bogus.' Maybe; it may very well be. But it can hardly be said that the distinction is made often enough to constitute a real barrier to progress in our time. Nor that there is not a prospect that in the future many lives will be nastier, more brutish and shorter than that of John Primatt Redcliffe-Maud.

# Public Schools *

WHEN in 1682, the Reverend Mr Busby, headmaster of Westminster School, expelled or suspended John Dryden's son, the poet wrote him an excellent letter. Busby had already been at Westminster for more than forty years: he was that terrifying thing, a Great Headmaster. Moreover, Dryden had himself been among his pupils and knew well enough what tricks the old autocrat could get up to. Busby had sent a message by the boy, that he 'desired to see' the father. Dryden hastened to assure him that his son 'did the message', but he did not obey the summons. His letter begins, indeed, by assuring Dr Busby that he would have come, if he could have found in himself 'a fitting temper', meaning, no doubt, that he was in no mood to talk to the headmaster as became an old pupil. His fury and his caution in addressing the great man jostle side by side throughout the letter. He admits or pretends that he found 'something of kindness' in the message, for Busby sent the boy away, so he said, in order that he 'might not have occasion to correct him' – a necessity more obvious, no doubt, to Busby than to the poet. He gives reasons why the boy's alleged crime was perhaps 'not so great' as Busby seemed to think. Then he tells the headmaster that his first impulse was to send for the boy's things from the college, without a moment's delay. That he did not do so was partly out of respect for Dr Busby and partly – and this clearly is the point of the sentence – out of 'tenderness of doeing anything offensive to my Lord Bishop of Rochester, as cheife Governour of the College'. A threat that the matter might not rest with the headmaster and that the chairman of the governors might hear of it. Dryden is

*John Rae, *Public School Revolution: Britain's Independent Schools 1964-1979* (Faber)

concerned that his son's chance of election to a university place will have been lost by the upset, and stoutly suggests the boy might as well go to Cambridge at once, 'of his own election'. The letter concludes with the hope that Dryden will be 'satisfyed with a favourable answer' from Dr Busby's 'goodnesse and moderation', so that he may continue his 'obliged humble servant', as, of course, every father with a boy at the school would wish to be.

A different world? Not at all, as regards the complex of essential relations between pupils, masters and parents. Manners have softened, and a twentieth-century headmaster who conducted himself towards the boys as Dr Busby did would probably be sent to prison for a noticeable time, as would, certainly, one who met an insurrection in the way Dr Smith – another headmaster of Westminster – did, at the end of the eighteenth century. He felled the ring-leader with a club. Dr John Rae, the author of this book and the present incumbent of the post held by Busby and Smith, assuredly has no thought of reviving past brutalities, though he admits, understandably enough, to thinking that some boys involved in contemporary troubles deserved to be hit on the head. As well think of bringing in the cavalry to ride down rioters in Toxteth or Brixton. Dr Rae is the thoroughly modern exponent of a gentleness which is probably no more highly thought of, by those who are exposed to it, than was the violence of earlier times. In a passage illustrating what he considers 'the most effective formula' for dealing with trouble in chapel – apparently the scene of various 'protests' in the Sixties – he gives what must be a sketch of his own methods:

> At the end of the service, the headmaster asked the visitors and the staff to leave. Alone with the school, he told them that he recognized that some of them had grievances, but that a mass protest in the presence of visitors was not the way to go about things. He avoided peevishness and sarcasm, the two qualities that would immediately alienate a schoolboy audience. He made no promises or threats. By removing the staff and speaking to the boys he had in one

simple gesture abolished the oppressive sense of hierarchy. They were his boys and he was their headmaster.

How touching! Did the boys really fall for that? If so, public schools must certainly be failing to instil an adult and critical attitude in their pupils. The sentence about 'removing the staff' will produce a laugh from people who have seen bosses in other circumstances try the personal touch at the expense of the intermediate management. The headmaster is alone with his illusions. He speaks directly to each of his overgrown charges while the staff, who are actually at death's grip with them, hour after hour and day after day, are supposed to represent 'hierarchy'. Well might Dr Rae suggest that 'public school headmasters are political animals'. But he is less than frank in his characterization of the species. 'Whatever other qualities of intellect and character they possess... they have stamina, an instinct for survival, a polite ruthlessness, a shrewd judgment of men and opportunities and a flair for identifying and, if need be, diverting the current of popular opinion.' What is missing is the admission that most of the time these talents have been exercised against immature persons. 'Fear of the boys is a potent factor. It could no more be admitted than a handful of British soldiers in a remote colonial outpost could admit they were afraid of the natives.' Things are not always as bad as at the critical moments of the Sixties to which these sentences refer, but it is these tribesmen who set the tone of the schoolmaster's operations.

Dr Rae does not mean us to attach too much importance to this aspect of the headmasters' activities. Indeed, his book is largely concerned with their tactics in defending their schools against 'inflation, political attack and social upheaval' – this last making a direct impact in the form of 'drug culture', 'pop culture', though not, thank God, 'punk culture', for that was a working-class phenomenon. (Dr Rae is full of 'cultures' – this manner of speaking is no doubt part of the evidence for the modernity he is so anxious to prove and, I would say, does prove.) His account of the public schools' response to the financial and political difficulties of 1964-79 takes us into worlds far beyond the schools themselves, but his approach is coloured by the world from which he issues forth. That he saw himself early in his career as one whose mission lay in the peripheral world of academic politics and bureaucracies is demonstrated by the fact that, while an assistant master at Harrow (his first job), he wrote to Crosland, who was then presiding over the Department of Education. He explained to the Secretary of State that he did not 'trust headmasters to represent the views of the rank and file'. How John Rae came to speak for those views is not clear. Crosland put him on to Reg Prentice, who saw him and was rewarded by a further letter suggesting that the membership of the current Public Schools Commission should include an assistant master and that he, Rae, was the man for the job. We all have to learn and this is not the best way to approach Whitehall on such a matter. But it was an opening gambit, and Rae's appointment a year later – in 1966 – as headmaster of Taunton School, and in 1970, when he was 39, as headmaster of Westminster, threw him into the public schools' own little political arena. In 1977 he was chairman of the Headmasters' Conference and, although 14 others must presumably have held the post as well as he, during the period he is discussing, Dr Rae can claim to have been at the centre of things.

Ah, but what is the centre, when it comes to politics? Not even the Headmasters' Conference, smartened up as it was in 1963 by the appointment of a consultant on public relations, who naturally advised 'more positive action in providing the public with a straightforward and up-to-date picture of public schools'. Not even ISIS (the Independent Schools Information Service), established in 1972, when the direct-grant schools had been destroyed and the public schools found it convenient to be known as 'independent schools', to make the most of the fact that they had been democratically reinforced by the considerable number of establishments which had been created out of the stubborn direct-grant schools which declined to be taken over. In fact, the necessity of entering the political field had – to judge by Dr Rae – so disoriented headmasters that they were hardly any longer the centre of anything, not even their own schools. For the preoccupation of proving the value and virtue of those establishments meant that, instead of having their minds on the schools, in the way that Dr Arnold had, they were distracted by thinking about the audience for their apologetics. It must be reckoned a come-down in the world to have to take seriously the menacing round face of Mr Roy Hattersley, putting it bluntly to a conference of independent-school headmasters: 'I must, above all else, leave you in no doubts about our serious intention initially to reduce and eventually to abolish private education in this country.' But even Mr Hattersley, portentous though he is and no doubt wishes to be, is not quite the centre either. Is there hope in Mrs Shirley Williams? I should not have thought so, given the extreme ambiguity of her actions and opinions, in the matter of education as in some others. However, you never know when you may need a friend or who that friend may be, and Dr Rae speaks of her 'intelligence, realism and lack of bigotry': all such praise is, after all, comparative.

One can understand that, the secondary, grammar and direct-grant schools having already fallen before the onslaught of politicians, the public schools – the independent schools – feel that they must now look out. Dr Rae is good on the divisions within the scholastic camp which have imperilled the defence hitherto. Schools have competed with one another for customers; more recently, boys' schools have raided the girls' schools. If, as the convinced exponent of the *Gleichschaltung* of education, the Labour Party has been the enemy, the Conservative Party could hardly be said to have been helpful. One has had the impression, over the years, that they knew little and cared less about the education of the lower middle classes or of that even more important part of the social substructure, the barely definable lowest middle classes whose day passed when it ceased to be possible for parents to buy a grammar-school education for a few pounds a year. Public schools the Conservative Party had certainly heard of, and not all of the inner circle went to Eton, though the Party has sometimes behaved as if they did. Anyhow, now that grammar schools (with few exceptions) and direct-grant schools have been abolished, and the average boarding fees for public schools stand at £3500 a year, it cannot be said that there is much choice left for the ordinary parent with an interest in literacy. One of the most significant questions, for those who concern themselves with the politics of these matters, is: who now goes to public schools? On this subject Dr Rae has some interesting things to say, though he is far less informative than one could have wished. 'By the end of the Seventies, it was rare to find an Anglican clergyman who could afford the fees of an independent school... as a significant group of parents the clergy disappeared.' (One must admit the fairness of the comment Dr Rae makes: 'that the tendency for Anglican priests to experience qualms of conscience about private education dates from the time when they could no longer afford to send their children.') But other significant groups of parents have appeared. Dr Rae mentions investment analysts, management consultants and 'many more who described themselves on their son's registration forms as "company director"'. One need have no special hostility to these three groups to feel that their prominence in this context is not entirely reassuring.

Even more worrying than the political threat to public schools is the economic threat, which this change of clientèle illustrates. But if the economic threat is severe, it is at least something that headmasters and school governors can do something about. A lot has been done. The widening of the basis for recruitment, including the admission of many beneficiaries of the Middle East oil trade and the pillaging of girls' schools for brighter pupils, has been part of the exercise of looking for the vastly increased fees wherever they can be found. The publicity put out to show that the schools had moved with the times may also be considered from this point of view: it has been more successful with the potential customers than with politicians. Even in the early Sixties the Headmasters' Conference was drawing up a list of the 'popular

myths that need to be scotched'. Some of them, like myths of
another kind, must rank at least has half-truths. The killing of
'myths' and the making of 'images' is anyhow at best a
secondary occupation: what really matters is what was done.
'Over £60 million' was raised in the years 1964-79, with the
help of fund-raising firms. The result has been that the public
schools have not only ceased to have 'barbaric living
conditions' and to teach 'no science' (h. and b. of the original
table of myths) but have become extremely well-equipped to
teach modern subjects. Dr Rae can cry lyrically: 'The time
British public-schoolboys once spent writing Latin verses is
now spent writing computer programmes.' How splendid!
How likely to appeal to the investment analyst and the
management consultant! How likely to appeal to the better-
paying employers, when the time comes to set out the *curriculum
vitae*!

Dr Rae is frank about the public schools' place in the
market: 'education was the service the schools were selling.'
Perhaps, like Mrs Thatcher, he has too exclusive a trust in the
market. He is so modern that one might say he has replaced Dr
Arnold, as the guiding star in the public school firmament, by
Walter Bagehot. And what, one must ask oneself, is he selling? I
should have to admit to being, in the end, scandalized by the
absence from this book of any real mark of concern for
education. It is not that I have any great faith in theorists of
education, remembering John Locke, who praised a mother
who whipped her daughter eight times before she subdued her,
on the grounds that had she stopped at the seventh occasion,
her daughter would have been ruined, and Rousseau, the
source of so many troubles, who was recklessly offhand about
the fate of his own children. But I cannot help thinking that
some schools may be better than others, and that the criteria
cannot be satisfactorily established by what the most well-off
parents are willing to pay by way of fees. Not that Dr Rae does
not point to the academic glories recognized in our time: '23
per cent of all pupils taking three or more A-levels are in
independent schools.' That is what parents will pay for, and

accounts for the diminished force of a. in the table of myths,
that public schools are 'a refuge for the brainless'. But Dr
Arnold was surely right when he 'strongly deprecated any
system which would encourage the notion' of academic
honours 'being the chief end to be answered by school
education'. Dr Rae seems not to have thought about 'the chief
end' at all: hardly, it sometimes seems, about the pupil, except
as a commodity. His subject is the public schools' 'extraordinary capacity for survival'. 'The headmasters of the Sixties
and Seventies often used the Christian foundation argument as
a means of discrediting Labour plans to take over their
schools.' It is an argument he thinks poorly of – which may be
right in the context, but that hardly affects its intrinsic merits,
one way or the other. There is much to be said for Christian
education; there is much to be said against sectarian schools,
the horrors of which are so apparent in Northern Ireland: but
neither issue has really surfaced in Dr Rae's mind. He sees
through the old cant; he falls for the new, neck and crop.
'Headmasters and new boys were on the same journey
searching for God in what appeared to be a godless world.' If
'in the Seventies the old assumptions about a Christian school
were no longer valid', neither, apparently, were the old
assumptions about the value of literacy. The study of Greek
and Latin in the sixth form became a highly 'eccentric
activity'.

What the public schools have preserved, through all the
social changes, is an ability to steer their pupils towards the
best university places and the best jobs. This valuable
characteristic is what parents are really willing to pay for. It
must have played a large part in the drift of girls into boys'
schools. Anyone who has sat on a selection board can imagine
the way the members would have brightened up when they
saw that the next candidate to be seen was one of the first girls
from Marlborough. By and large, there is, in the high places of
universities – not *only* in Oxford and Cambridge – in the Civil
Service and in industry, a strong sense of succession which is
linked to well-known academic establishments and to the

manners and outlook they promote: it is tempered only by a desperate desire to show a broadmindedness which would exclude such influences. This is what excites the political hostility towards public schools. It is no good arguing that liberty matters more than equality or fraternity, because it is equality that democratic politics are about, however little there may be of it in the real world. For anyone who really believes that privilege can be abolished by a political revolution – and that it does not just change hands, as more disillusioned persons think – it is difficult to see what argument is left in favour of public schools. If, on the other hand, one thinks that privileged groups, with much the same rapacious intent, form themselves in all societies, and that those of a socialist world are likely to be no more amiable, and perhaps less various, than those which can lay hands on the money now, one will not join in any witch hunt. In real life, parents with children to educate look around to see what is the best they can do for them, and the best teaching is no doubt in schools, however financed, where there are a few really good teachers. General remedies are the devil in education, and, of course, they are the only kind known to politicians. Anyone interested in the politics of education should consider what Dr Rae has to say: others should look elsewhere. I started to read this book thinking that I should at last find out what the Public School Question really is. Now I wonder whether there is one, apart from the social dreams of Roy Hattersley and Neil Kinnock. The public schools seem as set as anyone on playing their part in the decline of education, as far as their superior resources allow. Admittedly, my view of the matter may rely too much on Dr Rae, for I have never set foot inside a public school, except once to borrow a book.

# Religion and Public Doctrine

'PEOPLE are fully alive to the danger of superstition in priests', wrote Lord Salisbury in 1876; '... in course of time they will find out that ... professors may be just as bad.' They have found out; that much progress must be allowed to the past hundred years. The question whose prejudice is bigger than whose, of course, remains, not only as between professors and priests, but between members of these classes severally. It is revealed by Maurice Cowling in *Religion and Public Doctrine in Modern England* ★ that this 'profoundly normative' back-biting goes on even among professional historians, however much we may have been inclined to believe in the objectivity of their studies and the evenness of their tempers. Beneath the 'placid malice' of professional history, we are told, 'conflict is continual, in magazines, lectures, supervisions, appointments committees and books, between four or five world-views which are not compatible with one another'. So much for our illusions, if we had them.

It cannot be often, however, that in embarking on 'an extensive work' of history the author gives us four hundred and fifty pages designed to elucidate the point of view from which he will be writing. That is what we get here. For this volume is 'preliminary' only. The main work – in how many volumes, we are not told – will be a history of 'the public doctrines which have been propagated in England in the last century and a half'. It cannot be said that the notion of 'a public doctrine' has yet emerged with utter clarity. We are told it is something which 'adumbrates the assumptions that constitute the

* Maurice Cowling, *Religion and Public Doctrine in Modern England* (Cambridge University Press)

framework' – rather on the lines of the House that Jack built – 'within which teaching, writing and public action are conducted'. More explicitly: 'In England all participants in the public realm have had a doctrine, whether they have known it or not. Almost all of them have had a doctrine about England, whether the subjects they have written or talked about have been English or not.' That more limited notion I begin to understand, or I think I do, though it does not achieve articulation in the present volume. And although what we have here is 'an examination of the author's relation to the events of which the main work will provide a history', it is a little difficult, in the absence of that main work, to have more than an impression of what events are indicated. They lie, clearly, in the field of those changes of which one aspect is the replacement of Christianity, in greater or less degree, by doctrines which are potentially or actually anti-Christian. What is before the reader is 'a discussion of thinkers who have helped' the author to understand the significance of the history with which he proposes to deal.

A curious bunch they are, these thinkers who have influenced him – curious as a bunch rather than as individuals. The first is A. N. Whitehead, whose conception of religion was everything that might be expected from a man of his generation who was the son of an Anglican clergyman, educated at a public school and Trinity College, Cambridge, and who as mathematician and philosopher collaborated with Bertrand Russell. It is a good touch of Maurice Cowling's to comment that 'Whitehead's respect for religion was spoken of with respect'. Cowling's second influential thinker is Toynbee, one of those boring minds which must be employed somehow – a man who chose a subject so vast that he evaporated into it, taking the world with him as he thought, though fortunately a few myopic people were left carrying on below. Toynbee was against any such notion as 'the exclusive nature of Christian claims', and may be said to have provided the theoretical basis for the Archbishop of Canterbury to approach the Ayatollah Khomeini as one religious leader to another, as well as for much more that eminent clerics get up to these days. Whitehead and Toynbee, we are told, were the baggage Cowling took to Cambridge as an undergraduate in 1943 with – rather oddly, it seems to me, for the time of day – scrapings of 'Belloc, Bergson, Shaw, Wordsworth, Macaulay and Carlyle'.

In his undergraduate period, which was split by three and a half years of army service, Cowling underwent the wholesome influence of 'Three Anglican Reactionaries' – Canon Charles Smyth, Kenneth Pickthorn, and the Edward Welbourne who became Master of Emmanuel – then of Eliot and David Knowles. The next phase of Cowling's opinions is represented in a third part of the book by Butterfield, Oakeshott, Collingwood and Churchill, all regarded as more or less subversive. The final phase and the fourth part of the book present us with Kedourie, Waugh, Salisbury and Enoch Powell, together with some fifty academics – from Stubbs to Edward Norman – whose biographies provide a rich fringe of footnotes.

It is an extraordinary performance, and surely a laborious and somewhat inelegant way of establishing 'the existence, and the importance of a field of study'. I cannot but wish that Cowling had instead introduced his forthcoming history with a single essay in which he would have drawn the various strands from his authors into a statement of his own conclusions. What he is concerned with is 'a reaction to the realization that a post- or anti-Christian doctrine not only exists but has gained ascendancy'. There must be people for whom this realization is a matter of astonishment but they represent a somewhat modest level of sophistication, given the intellectual history of the past four hundred years. The bite is in Cowling's qualification that the ascendancy has been achieved in the era of 'universal suffrage and universal education'.

These developments have of course changed the operation of public doctrine in every field, and in every field that is a matter of scandal to some. There is no reason to quarrel with Cowling's assertion that 'Christian Conservation is . . . an instrument of investigation, a tool with which to approach the foundations of modern thought and the limitations of modern thinking', but it must be added that it is a useful tool just in so far as it manages to say something about these matters in terms which mean something to those who do not share the general view of the world it implies. This has, presumably, always been the problem of Christian apologetics.

The doubt which assails one, at this stage of Maurice Cowling's exercise, is whether he has that degree of openness of mind which successful apologetics require. The vulgar *will* believe that if they are to subscribe to Christianity it ought to be true in some sense of what they ordinarily mean by saying that things are true, and there is a huge task to be undertaken by theologians before that can be widely the case. Meanwhile, many of those who 'profess and call themselves Christians' – in the modest phrase of the now discarded Prayer Book – naturally stretch out their hands to supports they believe to be publicly recognized as valid, including some of those which Edward Norman and others think they have the best of reasons for denouncing. For public recognition is one of the most powerful criteria of the truth, the ability to see a church by daylight being something, after all. In a profound sense, the truth is what we would all agree about if only we could be made to see it. Cowling's collection of mentors leaves one uneasy. It is not only the disproportion of academics, one might say of Cambridge men; it is also the curiously hedged sensibility, and in particular of social sensibility, suggested by the prominence of figures more or less acceptable in a fairly closed middle-class world, who in spite of their worthiness and abilities, must be classed as less than first-rate by any wider standards, though there are, admittedly, also such people as Oakeshott and Kedourie. And what are we to make of a man who finds in Waugh illumination on the relationship between religion and society? Or who finds that Enoch Powell demands attention in this first volume as he will undoubtedly demand it later? What strange orientation makes Cowling see Churchill's influence on what the English 'wished to believe about themselves' as brought about 'to a far greater extent through his books' than 'by his public presence'?

There is a certain bookishness about Cowling's approach to

subjects which call for a wider sensibility; in the case of Eliot, his understanding of his subject is defective not only through lack of sympathy but through lack of information. It cannot be the case that Eliot 'had begun to pick up Maurras' in the 1920s, as 'in the thirties he picked up Christopher Dawson, Demant, Mairet, Maurice Reckitt and Karl Mannheim'. The influence of Maurras was incomparably more radical than that of the others, and it must date from the year Eliot spent in Paris around 1910. The reference to the 'Rev.' Maurice Reckitt and the casual allusion to Philip Mairet suggest that Cowling has some more work to do, before his second volume, on the later Eliot's connections with the world of Anglican sociology. The real trouble, however, seems to be that, in seeing Eliot primarily as 'an influential variant' of a 'type of Anglicanism' – that represented by the 'Three Anglican Reactionaries' – Cowling has missed most of the man, as a curious piece of pontification about the poems shows that he has entirely missed the poet. (The poet he really warms to seems to be the pre-war Enoch Powell whose work 'registered the resigned, masculine gloom of the Trinity ethos'. Perhaps that is unfair, but clumsiness about poetry is significant in the elusive studies Cowling is attempting.)

That the Christian religion, at any rate in its public manifestations, is in decline in England as in other Western countries is hardly deniable. There are those who manage to see improved private devotions as counter-balancing the overt decline, but they are rather like those who saw an increase in 'moral influence' which was to follow the demise of the Empire. It is certain that, unless Christianity has its own flourishing institutions, fewer and fewer people will find themselves in a position to know what that religion is. Not only have many individual pieties found a place within institutions of a certain worldliness, but the most recessed and fugitive devotions are strictly unthinkable without such institutions. Someone has to do the dirty work. So the question of public doctrine is very much a question of institutions, and of 'a doctrine about England' much more explicit than anything that emerges from Cowling's first volume. The recession from Christianity which Salisbury witnessed, not without a thought for 'the holders of accumulated capital', has gone far since his day and has been widely welcomed. The universities and most schools have been completely secularized, or carry residual traces so faint as not to affect their general character. The rate of dissolution has been much accelerated by the media, now really the *only* institutions which have massive public influence, and which convert religion as well as political events, 'the arts', and all particular knowledge and expertise to the purposes of a power-ridden entertainment world.

Edward Norman has spoken of the 'withering away of the ecclesiastical parts of the constitution', which is evident enough; the question now is rather whether, under the influence of pseudo-populist conceptions (all populist conceptions are inevitably pseudo), the whole constitution is now being dissolved. The processes involved in that, too, may be sure of a wide welcome, though it does not follow that they will bring in an age of contentment.

There is a sense in which those well-established middle-class university gents, Toynbee and Collingwood, may be said to have been prophets of the dissolution now being effected by the media, which are really superseding universal suffrage as a solvent. Toynbee's whole conception of a 'unified world' and 'superseding nationalism' were such as to distract attention from the actual problems of now and above all of here, and one may regret that he did not choose some field of operation less malleable than history. Perhaps – as he might easily have done – he should have become a civil servant, when he could have used his industry on no worse objective than plans even more grandiose than those of the late Lord Armstrong for the inflation of Whitehall. Collingwood's ' "infinite world", in which every fact was included,' is merely an unrestrained version of the media-man's lie about bringing the world to your doorstep. As Cowling says, 'the claim that universal history was essential in theory and impossible in practice raised important difficulties'. Well, it would. Similar difficulties have

been encountered by more practical post-Hegelians, who have
by sleight of hand managed to read the universe in the light of
their local and immediate interests, and indeed the
universality claimed for Christianity poses comparable
problems.

A local habitation and a name are, however, of the essence of
Christianity, though its exponents are always rushing off into
more or less wild abstractions, and 'a doctrine of England' is
not necessarily an absurdity. Such a doctrine was expressed in
the Book of Common Prayer, which saw 'this realm of
England' as a sovereign place which admitted the wiles of no
foreign administration. As regards the general affairs of the
kingdom, this did not need to be spelt out; as regards
ecclesiastical affairs, it was thought necessary to make the point
that 'the Bishop of Rome hath no jurisdiction'. Religion being
merely the truth, as revealed, there seemed no reason to
suppose that it would be better understood across the Channel
or across the Alps, and indeed there was thought to be some
evidence to the contrary. This did not mean that the King or
the Archbishop had replaced the Pope; it meant simply that
the Pope had not been replaced and was a superfluity. Of
course various worldly matters which Rome had dealt with
had to be dealt with somehow. The Church of England seems
to have lost confidence in the arrangements that were then
made, and many of her more innocent clergy and laity even
talk as if Louis XIV did not meddle with ecclesiastical
appointments and as if Rome itself was not a political
institution.

The assumption of the Book of Common Prayer was the
medieval one that members of the state were also members of
the Church – a point which it was not unreasonable to
reinforce at a time when the Reformation was bringing
bloodshed into every country in Europe, through circumstances of which the affairs of Ireland are a late and lamentable
example. A subject might 'wear weapons, and serve in the
wars' – as Christians had always done – but only 'at the
commandment of the Magistrate', and that meant under the

English Crown. There were prayers for the King, as there had been before the Reformation, and as elsewhere Roman Catholics prayed for the Emperor. By the time of the slightly florid additions to the book in 1662, the prayer was that the King might 'vanquish and overcome all his enemies', and no nonsense.

A notable peculiarity of Prayer Book Anglicanism, as compared with what goes on at the present, is that it provided a milieu for the devotions of Englishmen, and for their instruction in the Christian faith, without providing a forum for anything that could be called 'Christian opinion'. The Englishman was expected to go out from the Church and play his part in the commonwealth as seemed best to him. We now have a Synod cackling on about this and that and pretending to give the opinion of the Church on various political issues – an unedifying display, though I am happy to say that I never met an Anglican who felt himself bound by what is said there.

There were, of course, some noises in Convocations and Church Assemblies in the past, but with the establishment of the Synod the Church of England has wilfully demoted itself from the station of a national Church, to which it is perhaps no longer called. Its voice has acquired a sectarian stridency. It is now only vestigially more in the commonwealth than one more organ of opinion, and a badly briefed one at that.

Having thus stepped down – out of deference, it must be supposed, to democratic opinion – the Church of England must find itself at a disadvantage as compared with more practised agitators, and it has failed to achieve the status of a dissident, without which much pressure cannot be exerted. Given the folly of many Anglican counsels, this may be as well; still, the advices of the authenticated dissidents are not always of the wisest either. The major ecclesiastical operator of this kind is the Roman Church, which has long practice in that role in this country and has long been fortified by an influx of Irish clergy. Its peculiarity is that it combines the role with a relatively authoritarian structure, and has a directorate outside the country and engaged in world-wide politics.

The politics have been given a new lease of life by a world in which the media favour the voices which address not so much *urbem* as *orbem*. No doubt the Papacy will burn its fingers with the democratic states as formerly with the Christian monarchies, and the media will in time make more use of its opportunities for destructive criticism in that quarter. Meanwhile, however, the Roman Church in this country is sitting relatively pretty. There are, of course, also the traditional English Protestant non-conformists, whose position is now much that of their parent Church of England, if rather less confused. Then there is a host of more or less Christian sects of different ancestry, for the most part relatively undisciplined socially as well as theologically. There are the Jews who have a long and complicated relationship, not always the happiest, with the historical Christian churches, and who also dispose of international aids, though without formal organization. There are Hindus and Muslims, again with more or less informal relations overseas, with complicated social problems but with undoubted potential status as minority groups to be listened to.

It is difficult, in these circumstances, to see how a 'Christian conservatism', as adumbrated in this volume, can arrive unaided at 'a doctrine of England', however well it may be fitted to expose 'the limits of modern thinking' – by which appears to be meant that congeries of liberal prejudices which is the nearest thing we have to a consensus. A state which cannot pick and choose among the religions practised by its members is already in search of another religion, and ours may be said to have found one already, in democracy. As a system of belief – or of self-evident public doctrine – this at least has the advantage of being held by most of the population, including the vast majority who practise none of the traditional religions and know or care almost nothing about any of them. That the religion of democracy is neither more scientific than any other, nor guarantees the continuance of democratic institutions, must afford opportunities to discredit it, though they have been little used at present by Christian bodies. However, the prospect of an ideological battle for the control of the state cannot be said to be attractive, whether the assault comes from nominal Christians or from nominal atheists. The examples of charity offered by the Russian Revolution as by the Reformation and Counter-Reformation are discouraging. Better, it might be thought, to hang on to an erroneous public doctrine which has just happened, or not to have too much public doctrine of any kind, if that were possible.

It is perhaps not possible, for no political balance was ever held for long. But those who do not believe in the encouragement of rage may well hold that concern for public doctrine should, so far as may be, give way to an examination of the facts. If the Christian religion is true, then the creed is among the facts; if it is not, not. The Johnsonian Tory, in an age of demoted Anglicanism, should be content to exercise a more than Roman patience in waiting for the facts to be recognized and the Church in this realm re-integrated. There is some explaining to do before that can happen. Politically, this quite imaginary Tory will ignore democracy as a faith and give his attention to the facts of the constitution. In a world in which slipshod discussion of affairs has become a primary form of entertainment, there can be few grounds for optimism. None the less, the fact that all government is in its nature monarchic, and that it is modified and informed, not *per*formed, by representative institutions, might surely become more patent than it is. And for 'a doctrine of England' it would be better to substitute 'the facts of England' – complex and confusing, like all facts, but of their nature less hard to seize than those of universal history or 'one world', and so offering better hope of a realistic perspective.

# An Abdication by the Church

HAVING now pushed aside the Book of Common Prayer, the Synod of the Church of England, in its session in March 1981, turned its attention to less important matters. For, although the full consequences are yet to appear, nothing could be more important, to the Church's continuing identity, than the Prayer Book. In their passion for style – a *modern* style, they were ill-informed enough to say – the authorities seem to have forgotten that for the Church to lose her corsets was to lose her shape. I dare say, however, that with their other ruling passion for a hasty ecumenicism, they welcomed this inelegance. The truth none the less is that the Prayer Book contains a whole system for living in the world – in this realm of England for which it is designed – and if one does not have that system one has to have another, and that other has not yet been adumbrated. No wonder so many ordinary Anglicans, men of no vision, are puzzled.

The meetings of Synod throw into uneasy prominence the ordinary corporate problems of the Church – the problems of politics and polity which the Prayer Book, put together under real pressures and not in the frivolous spirit of so many current reforms, solved so deftly that the business of re-defining them in the contemporary context has been funked or perhaps merely ignored. Of course the loosening of ties with the state has long been gleefully welcomed by those who see in the growing dissociation a mark of sanctity as well as of liberty, but the giggling should be suppressed for things are not as simple as that. This church is still called the Church of England and one might have some reservations about the exuberance of the Bishop of Guildford, for whom 'what is becoming important on the world scene is also appropriate in England'. A little more admission of myopia might bring discussions nearer the ground.

The political fallacy which rages most strongly in this recently-liberated – or recently disoriented – Church of England is that there is or might be such a thing as a church without political trammels. One might say, with all deference to Thomas à Becket, that this notion of a possible independence of the church is but a version, writ horribly large, of the extreme liberal fallacy that individual opinion is always right and the state is always wrong. The most ineluctable of political trammels, however, are not those laid upon churches by the state but those they are subject to merely because of their nature as institutions. There is no acting as a body without acting politically. There are the horrors of internal government, exemplified in the Synod itself, and one need do no more than point to a remark of the Bishop of Truro – certainly one of the most clear-headed of the bench of bishops – in the course of the present session: 'The matter before us cannot be settled by the counting of heads.' The counting of heads must always threaten to drive the Church to compromise – a situation which may be well enough for a lay government, which tries merely to get by, but which must raise rather fundamental questions about the real nature of a body which has more august pretensions.

Of course, difficulties of this kind are not peculiar to the Church of England or its Synod, but these institutions are peculiarly vulnerable because they have committed themselves to the absurdity of a largely democratic assembly giving itself the airs of a government – rather as if the House of Commons tried to function without Crown or Ministers or government departments. That such a body is more or less at the mercy of the bureaucrats and committee-men operating in the neighbourhood must be obvious, and no doubt a little plotting with Church House helps on causes whether good or bad. There are also inescapable external complications about the Church of England's position as a political body, and these show up comically in relation to our Big Brother the Pope. For while the Church of England has been busy demoting itself to the status of a sect, the Pope has been exploiting the possibilities the media offer to his far-flung empire in order to strengthen his political impact to a point which would have been sharply contested in the days when there were Catholic monarchies to recognize the power struggle for what it is. Well might *The Times,* a paper not notoriously critical of papal manoeuvres, report that 'there was general agreement' in Synod that the Pope's visit 'was an occasion for warmth rather than for euphoria'.

Of the subjects which engaged the Synod at this session, the most important was, unquestionably, that of the proposals for a covenant with the Methodist, United Reformed and Moravian churches. The Synod's characteristic conclusion was to authorize a further step in the direction proposed, but not by a majority which would have left the final outcome beyond reasonable doubt. An interesting feature of this debate was the appeal by the Bishop of Guildford, in a speech which apparently did not mention the Prayer Book, to the authority of the Alternative Service Book – that mistress who has been introduced into the house doing the honours while the lawful wife was locked in her private sitting-room. The outsider could only gather that the Church of England has abandoned its claim to be the historic Church in this kingdom, and that the social separatism of the Reformed and Methodist bodies has with the passage of time given them a theological justification which would have surprised the Wesleys. It is rather as if the Church of England itself claimed no historical lineage further back than the administrative separation from Rome in the sixteenth century, or as if it were determined in the interests of equality and fraternity to make nothing of it. It all seems very odd, and the scheme bears the marks of opportunist botching, even if that botching now has quite a history of its own. Perhaps at the back of some of the protagonists' minds is a dubious identification of 'visible' with administrative unity, and surely it is strange that, at a time when the Church of

England is further than it ever was from making plain to its ordinary members what it believes, it should propose the assimilation of greater uncertainties. The mirage of '1,000 million people of many different races and cultures' said to be 'baptised members of the body of Christ' is perhaps distracting to those engaged in local business. Still, the question of what people here and now actually know and believe is of some importance, if a church is a congregation of faithful people. One cannot but have sympathy for the minority in Synod who cannot accept the separation of questions of order and arrangement from matters of faith.

Apart from the proposals for a covenant with Protestant dissenters, the main subjects discussed at this session of Synod were some matters of ecclesiastical discipline in relation to marriage, and a report of the Church's Board on Homosexual Relations. That neither subject was regarded as ready for definitive treatment need surprise no one. A cynic might say that what the Church is asking itself, in a complicated way, is whether it should follow the drift of the times, and if so how fast. Every precaution is required, for these are concerns in which people are most ready to prefer themselves to the Church. It is not so much what people do, as what they say about it, that has changed with the century. The standard of acceptability in the past could seem to emanate from the Church, but it is now clear to everyone that the real determinant is social practice. Where does that leave the Church? No polite person now refers to extra-marital relations of any stability as fornication, but what exactly is one to make of a service of blessing – as talked of and to some extent actually used – for what must be ranked ecclesiastically as second class cohabitations? It is just kindness, perhaps, and that is something, as those outside the Church would be the first to admit, in their Pelagian way. So conscious of fashion has the Church become, in sexual as in other matters, that many are left wondering whether it is not so much set against the world as following the world's teaching, but at a respectful distance.

# A Gentle Warning

A BILL designed to secure that, subject to certain conditions, at least one main service a month, in Church of England parishes, should be in the form prescribed by the Book of Common Prayer, is certainly an absurdity. It is absurd, almost everyone will say, at this time of day that Parliament should be asked to regulate what the parsons get up to on Sunday mornings. Members of Parliament thought they had washed their hands of such things in 1974, and that was late enough in the day. The promoters of the Bill which had its successful reading on 8 April 1981, and is to have a second reading this week, are, however, by no means so ingenuous as might appear. The first reading of the Bill attracted a degree of attention – and of parliamentary attendance – which few can have expected. The promoters were thus able to demonstrate that, far from being out of touch with the times, they had a real political sense of what is important to people. There was great ecclesiastical indignation, on the grounds that the matter was important only to a *minority* – which would be an odd and unsatisfactory reason for Parliament *not* concerning itself with any subject. It may be added that the assertion that Anglicans who want the Prayer Book are a minority within the Church is – well, just an assertion.

The more solemn reason given for the indignation of Synod-loving Anglicans (*they,* surely, are a minority!) is of course that the regulation of church affairs was put into the hands of the Synod in 1974 and that unsanctified parliamentary hands should no longer touch such matters. One can understand these sentiments on the part of those who thought they had climbed into the Synod as into a space-ship, and pulled up the ladder, but whatever the impression of those inside, such vehicles are controlled from the ground. The privileges Parliament gives, it can certainly take away. It beseems the authorities of the Church of England to remember that in the country at large their membership, however reckoned, is now a minority, and they should not expect from the public a respect they are not prepared to accord to serious elements within their own circles or outside.

It would certainly have surprised the ordinary churchgoer, in 1974, to learn that what was being plotted under the guise of a measure to allow the Church to manage its own affairs, was a complete change in the character of the Church of England. Concern was expressed at the time, by some of the more wary, about the possible fate of the Book of Common Prayer, and even as late as last year, when the Alternative Service Book was going through its final stages in the Synod, assurances were given that the Prayer Book still stood, and that no one therefore should lament its loss. The assurances were, frankly, a pack cf lies, and indeed the conduct of the ecclesiastical authorities at large, in relation to the Alternative Service Book, has been of a kind which would have been unsparingly blasted by any political opposition, if anything so disingenuous were practised – as who shall say it has not sometimes been? – by a government. Nothing could have illustrated better the inept and unhealthy cosiness of the Synod than their utter ignoring of the petition presented to them on the initiative of Professor David Martin. No one expected the *fauteurs* of the Alternative Service Book to turn tail at the sight of the petition, but that the petition should have been utterly ignored, that no reply of any kind should have been thought necessary, could only be taken to mark a determination on the part of bishops and clergy, to say nothing of the lay ecclesiastical politicians, to turn their backs on responsible outside opinion and behave as if they were a congregation of saints who had no need to notice the vulgar and the damned. That the petition was largely representative of educated opinion, literate and musical, meant that the Synod were in fact turning their backs on that alliance with learning which was one of the glories of the English Church in better days. No wonder the Alternative Book is what it is.

Now that the Alternative Book has been promulgated and widely distributed and the Prayer Book in most places pushed into corners, it is apparently thought safe to be honest. We find, for example, the *Carlisle Diocesan News* saying: 'Diplomacy may have required the unglamorous definition – "Alternative Service Book" – but the truth is that an alternative liturgy is a contradiction in terms... It is time therefore to abandon political tactics and cover-up titles which suggest that this is no more than an alternative, and that 1662 stands unscathed.' So the people of England have been kidded by these scruffy ecclesiastical politicians, and are now reckoned of so little account, in the Councils of the Church, that the little joke can be admitted. No wonder it was felt, when the petition was presented to the Synod, that the presence of outsiders of any sophistication would be an embarrassment. 'For our health's sake,' says the encyclical from Carlisle, 'the blood must be changed.' (The blood is that contaminated by the Book of Common Prayer.) 'What matters now is that the operation should be swift and complete.'

Time for Parliament to intervene? I think it is. Indeed, one may say that the Church of England has begun its course of synodical government by an affront not only to many of its members but to Parliament itself. For did not the authorities of the Church take on the new form of government well knowing, in their inner councils, what they would get up to, but carefully concealing the drift of their politics? Of course neither the promoters of the present Bill, nor those who support it from a distance, expect it to pass into law, and one can imagine the Government being more than a little worried if it faced that possibility. So far from wanting to meddle in such things, the State is delighted not to have to do so. None the less, in the last resort, if clerics are silly enough, in ordinary political terms, if they are dishonest and reckless, they cannot in the end escape retribution from Parliament. That, be it said, goes for other bodies besides the Church of England; it is *not* a peculiarity of the Establishment. For Parliament can do as it likes, and will do, if sufficiently moved. It may be that people now think that the old conflicts between Church and State are something only to be read about in history books. Not at all, as even a short political memory will show. Perhaps it is only in foreign countries, in France or in Poland, that such conflicts can happen? Not at all. We may be sure that, in the last resort, the country which, of all others, roused itself to throw off a foreign ecclesiastical administration and to work out a series of settlements which gave us, after all, a decent history of political liberty, will not stand more than a certain amount of nonsense in the name of religion, whether from the Moonies or anyone else.

The Prayer Book (Protection) Bill is the gentlest of warnings.

# Notes on Church and State

## I

THE Thirty-Nine Articles are rather unfashionable reading, but they are very good reading none the less. They are, of course, much spat upon by Anglicans these days, like other monuments of the English Church. As to their theology, Newman thought he had proved that they were in accordance with the Council of Trent, while generations of more Protestant persons have – shall we say? – taken another view of the matter. It could be argued that their theology is eirenic, if confused. It is not, however, my purpose to engage in polemics in matters so far above my head. What I should like to draw attention to is the politics of the Articles, of which it can be said that, at the least, they are no more inept than some recent inventions in this field.

One has to turn over several theological pages to come to: 'XXXVII. Of the Civil Magistrates.' 'The Queen's Majesty,' we read, 'hath the chief power in this Realm of *England,* and other her Dominions' – and the article goes on to make it clear that that does not let out the clergy, notorious through the centuries for claiming various privileges for themselves, as well worldly as spiritual, it may be said. To drive home the point with a minatory look at the chief contender for such privileges, the article concludes, that the 'chief Government . . . is not, nor ought to be, subject to any foreign jurisdiction'. It seems a bold claim, in an England continually open to a seepage of regulations from Brussels and elsewhere, but the Articles were conceived in the more youthful and confident days of the National State.

Article XXXVII, which is one of the longest, goes on to explain that what is at issue is not the government meddling with 'God's Word, or... the Sacraments'. No, it is to keep the upper hand on 'all estates and degrees... whether they be Ecclesiastical or Temporal'. And quite right too, one might think, with one's mind on what used to be called the peace of the realm. Or, quite wrong, with one's mind not on old ecclesiastical quarrels but on international courts of Human Rights and such-like fantasies of the contemporary imagination.

These would have been strange new perspectives for the authors of the Thirty-Nine Articles, and they would have asked, very reasonably, what powers upheld these non-domestic authorities? Where, they would have said, still thinking ineptly of the Prince of This World in Rome, was the crowned head which nurtured these pretensions against Her Majesty? While this question might not be altogether so foolish as the political circumstances of the present age might at first lead us to suppose, the contemporary answer would have been profoundly shocking to the questioners. If the suspected crowned head was not to be found, were the distributed Powers of Darkness to which such international authorities owed their authority not to be regarded as even more sinister? They had their agents everywhere, worse than the Jesuit priests who, in Elizabeth's reign, were after all deliberately treasonable, like the agents of Moscow in the twentieth century.

This is not the place to examine the immense web of documents and justifications which maintain the human rights industry as a powerful international cartel, more or less beneficial, more or less not so, like most such cartels. What would really have shocked the Tudor politicians would have been to discover that it was not these organizations as such, their princes, directors and judges, which or who, in the last analysis, claimed this superb authority on earth, but that these authorities pointed away from themselves to the voices and consciences of mankind at large. This would have puzzled them because they would not at once have seen how the testimony of all these consciences could have been collected and reconciled – a good question. It would also have worried them because, although themselves passing as the supporters of the individual conscience, up to a point, they had not intended that things should go so far. The Roman authority notoriously and, they thought, erroneously pointed away from itself to a divine commission. No sooner get away from that false claim, they would have said, than we find authorities pointing to a human commission which was hardly distinguishable from a mob.

We who understand the refinements of democratic machinery – or who have accustomed ourselves to behave as if we did – know that there are methods of ordering and civilizing the individual opinions which would otherwise make up a mob and extracting from them something which resembles due process of government. We could laugh at our Tudor forebears and assure them that, rotten though our governments might be, they had many sophistications unknown to earlier ages and indeed managed to avoid some rather rough Tudor habits. We should also have to point out that the Protestant revolution had been so successful – more successful than either the Tudors or the Stuarts intended – that in our sort of state religion itself had become wholly a matter of individual conscience, though some people restricted their consciences in deference to an authority they had chosen for themselves. Humph! the Tudor statesmen might have said, thinking still of that Bishop of Rome who, they declared, had 'no jurisdiction in this realm of England', as well as of sundry tumultuous conventicles with which they had had trouble.

The authors of the Articles did not go too deeply into this question of liberty of conscience, which it would have been difficult to do after thirty-six articles dealing with points of ecclesiastical doctrine. They did, however, treat briefly, in the remaining paragraphs, with one or two matters of conscience which had given some trouble from Anabaptists and the like. 'The laws of the Realm may punish Christian men with death, for heinous and grievous offences', they said, discreetly leaving it to the civil laws to say what offences were so considered. They were not for any interference with the traditional dissuasives from public disorder. Nor would they brook awkward questions of conscience about the defence of the realm: 'It is lawful for Christian men, at the commandment of the Magistrate, to wear weapons, and serve in the wars.' Note, however, the moderation of this claim. They had no need to think of a universal conscription, of the kind familiar to us since the epoch of liberty opened by the French Revolution. They did not assert a positive Christian duty to bear arms, which would have raised intractable questions about the clergy. It must not be assumed that they were thinking of a modern liberalism in relation to the laity, for a very moderate Anglican divine of the Stuart century said that "tis pity but that his neck should hang in suspence with his Conscience that doubts to fight' when his country is invaded and that 'in offensive war, though the case be harder, the common Soldier is not to dispute, but do his Prince's command.' The contemporary state so far admits the existence of an unprovable conscience as to allow objection on general pacifist grounds – mainly, no doubt, in spite of the patter to the contrary, because there is less trouble that way.

A more ticklish point – though theoretically only, for it has nothing to do with modern economic arguments – is the question of property. The authors of the Articles, concerned no doubt for the propertied classes but also for the only form of public order they could conceive, boldly asserted that 'the Riches and Goods of Christians are not common, as touching the right, title and possession of the same'. That was what 'certain Anabaptists' did 'vainly boast'. With their minds on the same disturbers of the public peace, the authors of the Articles also asserted that, 'when the Magistrate requireth, ... so it be done ... in justice, judgement and truth', a man might swear on oath in a court of law – another disputed point. This little difficulty has naturally disappeared as, in deference to conscience, the respectability of mere affirmation has grown.

## II

Conscience is a very sophisticated conception, but it can also be a very simple one. A casuist may think condescendingly of a conscience not instructed by himself; some highly instructed persons – Pascal for one – have thought some casuists rather funny and rather dishonest. But what all consciences have in common is that they have been *taught,* more or less. They are a product of our civilization and barbarisms, as well as of the controverted residue which was there 'originally', whatever that might mean. So the conscience of the world, so frequently reported in the media to be 'affronted' by this or that, is a rather suspect article. Who taught it? one must wonder.

Indeed all consciences are suspect, as the Church has been among the first to point out. The mind of man is infinitely devious, and claims to purity of intention are to be taken with a pinch of salt. That of course goes for ecclesiastics as well as for the rest of the world. There is nothing more difficult to impart, surely, than the divine residuum of which they claim to be the exponents. The statement of doctrine has, traditionally, been hedged with many precautions, none of which has given universal and unqualified satisfaction. Be that as it may, the application of doctrine, the appreciation of its consequences in the field of action, has proved a treacherous one for all concerned. There is a vast area of ecclesiastical pronouncements which a reasonable man may regard with suspicion. 'The Church of Rome hath erred,' – the *Thirty-Nine Articles* declares – all particular churches have erred: that is certainly the commonsense of the matter as relating to all ordinary ecclesiastical pronouncements, whatever may be the case as to the ultimate residuum of doctrine. The ordinary victim of ecclesiastical guidance is in an uncertain position, like the rest of us, when it comes to taking a view on the affairs of the world, if only because information is a part of the truth and ecclesiastical information has not always been all it might have been.

Whatever may be the quality of the guidance afforded it, no one disputes that the conscience is an individual faculty, to be exercised as best we can in the face of all the evidences and instruction presented to it. How far we should listen to father before we decide – and indeed, who *is* father – are questions at the bottom of all the argument which has gone on on the subject in recent centuries: all that is distinctly at the sophisticated end of the range of conceptions of 'conscience' now prevailing in the world at large. The range extends far outside the world of theological conceptions – or of what is commonly understood by them.

For Machiavelli a mask of religion, on a competent politician, was likely to be – precisely – a mask; and wily men have always been suspicious of eloquence. But the great popular success of 'conscience', from the Reformation, through the vainly boasting Anabaptists and the like to Voltaire, Rousseau, the French Revolution and beyond, has delivered into the hands of politicians an armoury of a more potent kind.

For we have long arrived at Democracy, somewhat fallible in its ordinary practice, as indeed imperfect in its organization, but generally said to be infallible in principle. If anything goes wrong, everyone agrees at once that there wasn't *enough* democracy. Have some more and everything will be all right. We have not been righteous enough, according to current conceptions, so the wrath of God – or some more popular substitute – is upon us. What we used to have, in this country, in the days when foreigners were misguided enough to imitate us, was a *mixed* government, royal, aristocratic and democratic. A mixed government is in fact not only the best sort to have, it is the only sort you *can* have, in the modern world. It is the right recipe for the mixture which is difficult. But the patter put out no longer says that. It says that governments – all decent governments – are 'democratic'; the various mechanisms which make them work in spite of being democratic are more or less ignored, more or less concealed, more or less denied. Yet who does not know that the tiniest organization –

let alone a modern government – will not work without one or two hard-bitten people who actually do things and take account of facts, as well as the uncertain number who stand around talking and expressing opinions which may or may not take account of the facts?

The centre of this mystery is the encouragement, by those who are elected, of belief in the magical nature of the process. Who elected you? is their question, which may be counted upon to floor any non-elected person who might come near to winning an argument merely on merits. Of course, in an appropriate constitutional context this is absolutely right, for arguments have to be ended somehow, so that the work can go on. But the constitutional context seems to matter less and less, for beyond the elected person is the individual voter, whose untiring conscience is perpetually to be probed to find an answer more correct than the correct answer that was found last time. Moreover, since elections unhappily don't take place quite *all* the time, even in the most sophisticated democracy, various ways have to be found of discovering what the oracles would be saying if they were asked to speak. And the obvious way is to ask them to speak, out of season as well as in. So we get various collectors of oracles, of varying degrees of professionalism and amateurism; their objective is to launch themselves on properly constituted governments waving documents which prove that on some point or other the official augurs are wrong, as indeed they frequently are, though it does not follow from that that any particular set of unofficial augurs is right.

'Two things fill my mind with ever-increasing wonder,' said Immanuel Kant, the highbrow exponent, if anyone ever was, of the Nordic Protestant conscience, 'the starry heavens above and the moral law within.' Kant's wonder might have increased still more if he could have seen the excesses of conscience in our day. What he had in mind was the solitary philosopher taking a dog for a walk. What we have to think of, in the context of contemporary politics, is a variety of persons not all in the same tradition. The old casuists had in mind a patient who would stop and listen to them, but our public will not stop to be instructed. The casuists were certainly right to make the point that the individual might often confuse what he thought was right with what he merely wanted; they omitted, in general, to add that the same might be true of the casuist. We have greatly simplified these matters, so far as politics are concerned. In democratic practice, as well as mythology, what you want and what you think should be done are one and the same thing. A conscience, ultimately, is a vote, and that is all there is to it.

In this historic migration of the conscience from religion to politics a strange metamorphosis has occurred. For the original question of conscience was, What should I do? The political question is, What should someone else do? In spite of some more unobtrusive activities going on here and there the Church, deferential as usual to the drift of the times, shows signs of following this political lead. Once we were invited to pray God 'to save and defend all Christian Kings, Princes and Governors', so that the established authorities could get on with their duties in accordance with *their* consciences. Now we are more likely to be asked to uphold alleged rights against the better judgment of some government or other, it may be that of the Queen's Majesty, over whom the bishops have now given themselves precedence as if they were common Anabaptists. They are making obeisance to the supreme power residing in the conscience of votes.

For the Roman church things are probably a little different. They have a long tradition of meddling in the affairs of lawful governments and take like a duck to water to the business of putting governments to rights. They even – though it is an absurdity – have their own diplomatic representatives.

### III

Democracy has in effect dis-infected the individual conscience of its sanctity, at the same time that it has made it the foundation of the state. For the conscience of mankind, that of a nation, of the 'communities' of which, in this country, the nation is allowed to be made up, is a collection of votes and it would be to succumb to the clap-trap of the system to suppose that it is any more. The historical prestige of the truly *individual* conscience – the theological and, to a less extent, the philosophical one – is for the moment enough for politicians to invoke it, but that is a sleight-of-hand. There is no collecting all the determinations people make for themselves, as to their own actions. What can be and is vociferously collected is *opinions* as to what someone else ought to be doing, and politicians of various descriptions offer themselves as instruments for giving effect to all that is finest and noblest, etc, and that can be made out, at a quick look, to be derived from the sacred fountains of individual reflection and individual devotion.

The politicians are by no mean confined to the constitutional machinery, or to what is left of it or has been added to it. Indeed it is arguable that, to an increasing extent, the elected members of political parties, operating at Westminster or in local government, more and more have to fall back into a role formerly occupied by the Civil Service, of responding to political pressures generated by more strident figures. It is as if, between the official politician and the individual opinions of his constituents, which he is supposed in some sort to represent, a whole new army of irresponsible operators had slid. It is to this ghostly and it might be said sinister set of unavowed politicians that the official politician has to bow; it is they who collect individual voices, or who speak directly to the voters. No wonder there is confusion. The situation is of course not entirely new – what social or political situation is? – but there is enough in it that is of relatively recent development for the reality of government to be much farther than before from its constitutional appearance. The influence of the media is much talked about, though certainly far from sufficiently accounted for, as yet. Spasmodic attention has been given to the operation of pressure groups. Our concern here is only with those pressure groups which wear the sheep's clothing of religious opinion.

Can these religious groups, churches, organizations more or less under more or less leaky ecclesiastical umbrellas, prophets invoking more or less clandestinely Divine Powers which are thought still to have a certain voting strength, really be wolves? The BBC runs, at 8.15 on Sunday mornings, an illuminating programme called *Sunday,* an appreciable part of which, each week, is given to statements for or against some currently debated political issue. The members of some church here, or some committee there, or some organization purporting to be of more religious intent than the rest of mankind, is put up to make out that 'Christians' or 'Christian opinion' is in favour of, or against – whatever it is in favour of, or against. Occasionally the view is supported by some sketchy argument with, let us say, theological connections. More often than not one is faced with mere assertion or, as they say, faith. It would be an undeserved compliment to the clarity of mind of many of the speakers to say that they are deliberately using a tried rhetoric to advance their particular political opinions, though here and there, no doubt, there are lucid politicians who deliberately use some 'Christian' organization as one more forum for their views. But, motives apart, the nature of the operation is to try to collect listeners who are, or imagine themselves to be, Christians, behind some bit of a programme which will have to be settled by governments or other properly constituted authorities of the state.

Why not? most of them would say, either in genuine astonishment or with the weary air of those accustomed to the prejudices (usually qualified, though with no great historical accuracy, as 'old-fashioned') of those who think 'the Church should not meddle in politics'. There are several theological answers to this question, all more or less debatable in these circles, no doubt. There is also a non-theological answer of some importance. This is, that it is not in terms of their 'Christian' appeal that the matters they raise will be settled. It is even wildly discriminatory (usually held by such speakers to be a damnable thing, in other contexts) to suggest that this or that religious opinion should have any particular weight in settling affairs of state. The arguments have to be in terms of money and interest – held to be universally valid counters – or of 'rights' which, whether imaginary or not, are so abstract as to be equally comprehensible, and of cognate, even identical, meaning for people of all races and cultures – for the 'conscience of mankind', you might say.

The churches themselves, it ought to be made plain, do not really exist, for democratic politics. This has of course been clear enough, on that remote continent of Europe, ever since the French Revolution. In this country the survival of certain constitutional arrangements, to say nothing of the lack of clarity in the intellectual atmosphere, has made it possible to contend – though with decreasing conviction – that 'Christian' opinion ought to count for something. In the countries where the social institutions of the Roman Church have survived best it has been necessary for politicians to make various overt arrangements with the Vatican, but that is a political story on its own. For democracy there can be no 'Christian opinion'; there are just opinions, and out of the resolution of these opinions, more or less imperfectly expressed, and the invincible facts so far as they are apprehended by governments, come the decisions which, for good or ill, governments take on our behalf. The opinions must – or we have unfair discrimination! – be valued not on the basis of their quality but of their number; it is that which has to decide. Admittedly most government decisions are in practice taken – perhaps happily – in ignorance of what 'most people', or even most of their party supporters, think about the matter in hand. And there are, to put it mildly, various ways of calculating a majority, so that the skilful operator in government is not as much trammelled as, on pure democratic theory, he should be. But an approach by an archbishop or a cardinal to the seats of power is quite rightly regarded with suspicion. Whom is he trying to kid? The only authority he has a right to invoke is that of his constituents, and their connection with him is, so far as political actions are concerned, a pretty phoney affair. In so far as he is listened to it is because he comes trailing votes, or because it might be worth inquiring whether he does.

The theory of vote-catching is, however, no more than the ultimate concern of politicians, the sanction which determines, for a time, whether they will be there or not, when the next caller comes. A more elusive but, in the end, more powerful consideration is the nature of the discourse in which public discussion of political issues is conducted. This is more and more determined in the melting pot of the media. To that extent no doubt the promoters of 'Christian opinion' (normally meaning that of that sector of the opinion of Christians which comes nearest to the 'Religion of Democracy', of which more hereafter) and 'Catholic opinion' (normally meaning a Roman-Irish mixture) are right in trying to get their voices heard in the confused jumble of broadcasting. Neither having anything to do with the devotions of the people, it perhaps does not matter that the best they can hope for is to leave traces on a process of decision-making which disowns theology altogether.

## IV

The pretence that politics is an affair of conscience is very seductive. It enables those who promote it to think well of themselves. It flatters those who support it, for they are told that they are virtuous too. And whatever the changes in manners which result in yesterday's scandals being today's respectabilities, people always like to be thought virtuous, it seems, even though they may shrink from any terminology they believe to be old-fashioned.

This is far from being altogether a bad thing, in political terms, for the survival of some form of collective prejudice is essential, for a society to survive – *any* society. The history of the prejudices now reigning in this country, and beyond, is at least as long as the history of Europe. In their present form these prejudices derive partly from the historical church, partly – and more largely – from post-Christian pagan sources which owe a good deal to ecclesiastical history. It is a commonplace that 'scientific' liberalism has more than a dash of Christianity in it, and that what is called 'humanism' is a post-Christian humanism. This makes the situation of the churches a rather complicated one, when they dabble in public affairs. The weaker heads in the ecclesiastical world are apt to see, in the 'rights' now bandied about so freely everywhere, an expression of what Christianity is 'really' about. More wily and sophisticated persons see a connection which may enable them to interest pagans in the doctrine of the church, which they assert is what the 'rights' are really about. Both are rearguard positions, so far as the historical church is concerned. They are a recognition that the churches are not among the socially or ideologically dominant forces, and that to obtain any sort of hearing in the public world they have to scream aloud – shouting with the best of them, so to speak.

Whether such loud and vulgar talk is possible, without denaturing the message they have to deliver, is for ecclesiastics to determine. If their predecessors spoke more genteelly, it is because they were more assured, socially, than can be the case today. 'A gentleman in every parish,' said Coleridge, singing the glories of the English establishment. That is not what we have nowadays nor, if we have, would the parson be listened to on account of such a social status, now discredited. Popes were – and as far as seems plausible, still are – much given to showing kings and other rulers that they should, in the last analysis, take their orders from the see of Peter – a point of view which Dante, and no doubt many others in that 'age of faith' as well as in less faithful ages, found to be a detestable enormity. The claim is merely the extreme example of the church – or its ecclesiastical establishment – keeping its end up with the world.

It is difficult to discuss these subjects without coming near to theological ground which I should wish to avoid and in particular to the whole range of questions about the nature of the church. Anglicans, as usual, have a disarming and ambiguous answer to begin with: 'The visible Church of Christ is a congregation of faithful men, in which the pure Word of God is preached, and the Sacraments be duly administered...'

(Article XIX), but that stops no one arguing and indeed such arguments can be stopped only by Authority – politically an aberrant notion, at least in our time; the notion of an authority defining itself is utterly unacceptable. Be that as it may, the church which 'keeps its end up' in the world, whether Roman, Orthodox or Protestant, does so by the most human of means. The judge in this matter is the world, which makes no bones about *its* own authority, however its constituent elements may bicker among themselves as to their share of it. What matters to the world at large is its prejudices, what matters to the political world is its votes. No doubt the Pope's advertising man, Mark McCormack, is bringing fresh enlightenment to the Vatican on these matters. The antics of men in funny hats, or in funny collars, and the degree to which these men pretend to or actually can influence the views of their constituents, are what matter to the world. The theological subtleties adumbrated in Article XIX are beside the point. And when the authorities of an ecclesiastical institution – whether Papal, Rastafarian or Anglican – speak on a matter of public interest, it matters neither more nor less than the support they can command. So the more long-lived of these institutions tend to take on the social characteristics of the age. The Papacy has been princely and vicious in its time; it now wears an altogether blander look and speaks of rights – a word whose meaning changes with the times. E. J. Delécluse in his *Journal* for 23 February 1826, tells how a young Roman who killed a prelate was '*émancipé*' by Leo XII; he was formally given some extra years (he was only 18) so that he could enjoy the benefits of capital punishment for which the lower age-limit in the Papal State was then 21. Emancipation in this sense has no doubt gone out of fashion in the Vatican.

The point is that a church, whatever its theology, must when it acts on the public scene take on the role of a political institution. The fewer practical responsibilities of its own it has, in any political field, the more respectable it will look. In the twentieth-century world, there has been a tendency for churches to confuse playing a sort of game with opinion with the prophetic role which they must be supposed to exercise without violence to their more intimate nature. Anyhow, even a genuine prophecy is only an opinion, when it comes on to the modern political scene. In emitting opinions churches are in some sort playing a political role; they are bodies elbowing around in the state and trying – like how many others! – to give events a twist which the unassisted electoral processes have failed to give them. Institutions engaged in such manoeuvres are a normal part of our society. The most notable are the TUC, and its constituent unions, and if general secretaries have an election at some point in their career to give them democratic legitimacy, they may in time come to speak with as much remoteness as any archbishop or cardinal.

With the Christian denominations which are now, so to speak, part of the advisory crowd on the public scene there are also Jews, Moslems, and Hindus to be considered. The Jews have been long established socially, so it is most often as a voice of conscience that they are heard, like the various Christian bodies. Because Moslems and Hindus – as groups, though of course by no means always as individuals, many of whom know all anyone need know about British ways – are still in the process of assimilation, they tend to appear in the public mind rather as racial than as religious groups. As far as they are public voices of conscience, they naturally couch their appeal in the vague generalities of 'world opinion' rather than in the traditional (near-Christian) language of this country. Muslims and Hindus have a delicate problem they in a manner share with Jews and Roman Catholics; that is the temptation to invoke the help of their brothers across the seas. While no one would wish to suppress this activity entirely, it has its dangers, for those who use it are helping themselves to an extra weapon not available to the ordinary irreligious, or even Protestant, native. This tends to direct attention away from the channels available to all citizens, and to encourage thoughtless people to represent the ordinary difficulties of social life as intolerable oppressions that call for the intervention of outsiders.

There is a danger that groups with what might be called

allies of conscience in other countries will exercise a disruptive
influence by claiming to be not merely a domestic body seeking
political influence but the representatives of a collectivity
which can assail the elected government waving the banner of
a foreign power, however discreetly. We are so used to this sort
of thing that the impropriety of it, in democratic terms, easily
escapes people. Things were clearer on the less crowded stage
of the nineteenth century. The first Roman Catholic peer to
take his seat in the House of Lords delivered himself of a
defence of drinking the Pope's health before the Queen's.
Surely this is a piece of ill-manners, or a mild sedition? It was
certainly in contradiction with Lord Arundell's main thesis
that the Pope's authority was of a wholly different *kind* from the
Queen's.

V

The Anglican view of politics, which has been so inconsider-
ately overturned by the authorities of the Church of England
without their putting anything in its place or, to all
appearances, having any idea what they were doing, is one of
great depth. The product of much conflict, it is characterized
by a great – some might say excessive – serenity. The Church of
England has always been 'unquestionably loyal', as Bishop
Ken said, and I cannot, myself, see anything wrong with that.

The Church of England is the Church in England – that is
the basis of the Elizabethan settlement which, admittedly, is
too *geographical* in conception for the modern world, to say
nothing of its being too undemocratic. The claim is essentially
the same as that which the Roman church still makes, when it
refuses – as at critical points it always does – anything like full
recognition to other churches. There has been an immense
Roman propaganda, since the sixteenth century, to deny the
historical continuity of the English church, and this is no place
to continue the brawls which this has occasioned. In any
ordinary sense of the word 'truth', the detail of all historical
claims to continuity, from wheresoever promulgated, is

riddled with lies anyway, which is not to say that there are not degrees of truth in this matter. Be that as it may, the old Anglican conception, like that of the wider mediaeval church, was that everyone was a member of the church and of the commonwealth, of the spiritual and the temporal communities. The difference is that before the Reformation there was an appeal to Rome, supposed to be upon spiritual matters, though most often the differences were on political and economic matters in which it was handy for the ecclesiastic concerned to call in a European authority who was as much a prince as any of them, whatever else he was or wasn't.

After the Reformation, the appeal stopped with the sovereign, and in course of time the control of the sovereign was taken over by constitutional processes – ultimately by the democratic controls we know. Throughout this process the Church of England had its ups and downs, including the years 1645-60 when it was an illegal, underground organization. As it chugged on after the Restoration, with more or less absurdity and decreasingly general acceptability, it remained, theological niceties apart, *the* Church in this land. It occupied the historic buildings; it baptized, married and buried most of our ancestors; for years it doled out the social security and in very recent times it was the rag-bag to which all ordinary soldiers not claiming some special dispensation were presumed to belong. Its ordinary members did not have the feeling of belonging to something special, but to something ordinary; they were the non-peculiar people. As such, they vaguely supported the establishment and were faintly bolshie about it. They were far from feeling any special duty to agree with the vicar, still less the bishop, and as for clinging together in a gang, in the way that non-conformists of various kinds, including Roman Catholics, might do, that never entered their heads. The slightly flabby tentacles of the church stretched out into the ordinary population, and it was by no means clear where they stopped. Of course this state of affairs has at various times been regarded as theologically scandalous by more than one party in the church, but they have only been parties and the ordinary untheological Englishman did not think a lot of them. With the sharp decline in the intellectual calibre of the clergy, which I am afraid must be admitted, its mere failure to recruit any sort of reasonable share of ordinarily able people, the strong intellectual case for the soggy middle – the historical case – fell by the wayside. It began to be thought that all intelligent people would be content with a new mixture made up largely of the follies and vanities of opposed and vocal ecclesiastical parties. This is, roughly speaking, the rubbish now enshrined in *The Alternative Service Book.*

What we have now, instead of a *via media,* is a sort of canting conspiracy of the more superficial elements in both ecclesiastical wings, a church of *opinion* rather than of fact and history. The bishops were careful to put themselves before the Queen, in *The Alternative Service Book,* for the first time publicly showing their jealousy of their Roman brothers. The political implications of this have been passed over in complete silence. Might it not call in question the propriety of the establishment? When at the last Synod a back-bench cleric put down a motion in favour of disestablishment, the bishops and whatever other authorities manipulate the strange body shuffled it to the end of the agenda, so that it should not be discussed. But of course the issue is there, and not only in the queer little display of pique over precedence. The whole tone of the Church of England is now that of a sect; we hear that 'the church thinks this' or 'churchmen think that' – news indeed to most ordinary members of the church, who did not think they had handed their opinions on public affairs over to those to whom God had no doubt given a special authority but not always, alas, a sense of the limits of their competence. The proper Anglican view of these matters, it cannot be often enough said, is that the church instructs its man, makes what it can of him in the circle of its devotions, and then leaves him to go out and play his part in the commonwealth as best he can and as his own peculiar knowledge and experience, whatever they may be, suggest.

Ecclesiastical authorities who think they can upset this sober and realistic arrangement without raising the question of disestablishment have got another think coming. They are claiming to be *a group with an opinion,* like any other, and like any other they will become. Why should Anglican bishops sit in the House of Lords, and not the Chief Rabbi? Is it certain that the religion of democracy most of them now favour – I mean that sentimentality about vulgar opinion which has come to be regarded as a sacred principle – will leave them in the House of Lords or in residences anachronistically called palaces? It is fortunate indeed that circumstances are such that the central question of the religion of the sovereign does not arise at the present time – as some enemies of the Church of England would certainly wish it to have done – for in the present utter disarray the Anglican contribution to the discussion would certainly be a pitiful one.

One hardly likes to suggest it, but perhaps the Anglican authorities should encourage some thought to be given to the political position of the church. They should start with the study of the not very trendy literature of passive obedience, to which some of the greatest names in the English church have contributed. It is the counterpart of the classic attitude of the English layman – the man who goes to church but forms his own opinions on public affairs including, of course, the public affairs of the church. George Berkeley was not a silly man, and what he had to say on the subject would make a good starting point. Was he not Bishop of Cloyne as well as being one of the greatest of English philosophers – in the older sense of the word English, no doubt? It would certainly sound strange, in a committee of Synod, to hear it maintained 'that there is an absolute unlimited non-resistance or passive obedience due to the supreme civil power, wherever placed in any nation'; or 'that loyalty is a Moral Duty, and disloyalty or rebellion, in the most strict and proper sense, a Vice, or breach of the Law of Nature'. Still, the experiment should be tried, and would surely do something for the sloppy intellectual atmosphere of the parent body.

The great refinement of the old Anglican system, in the matter of politics, is that it neutralizes entirely the position of the church as an organ of opinion, and any disposition of its members to form a gang, leaving it to the individual subject and citizen, oriented as far as may be by historical Christianity, to play his part in the commonwealth as seems good to him. No man can do more, and a man who takes a certain view of public affairs *because* a bishop or any other ecclesiastical authority so suggests, is doing less.

# VI

It was asserted by Blackstone that Christianity is part of the laws of England, but it has to be admitted that things have changed since 1765. Nor is it true, as was suggested recently in the correspondence columns of the *Spectator* (11 July 1981), that it is 'far simpler . . . for civil authorities to consider the truth of any religious teaching rather than pretend they are all of equal worth'. The subject is not simple at all. Macchiavelli may be consulted as to some of the difficulties of past practice. In a modern democratic state, it is not the truth that matters, but the number of people who share any particular beliefs, whether deluded or not. And the *suprema lex,* whether in despotism or democracy, is the *salus reipublicae,* the mere continuation of the state, a matter rarely mentioned in decent society, like some other matters, but there all the same.

The practical problem, in England today, is how things should be arranged in a society which is residually Christian and which still has the church built into its non-representative institutions, but in which the representative institutions, where the effective power lies, are bound to ignore religion except as an element in opinion. As an element of opinion, Christianity, in a variety of forms, is still dominant, but there are Jews, Muslims and Hindus to be considered. There is also the vast mass of the population who now understand that religion no longer confers respectability and who therefore do not mind what happens to it, as well as the active minority who, following Karl Marx or Voltaire, or some other modern figure, think it should be abolished. All these opinions are equal, as far as our political institutions are concerned; even bishops, in their constitutional capacity, have to take account of this fact. The sovereign is not the sovereign only of Christians, still less only of Anglicans. Indeed while in the sixteenth century it was said that the religion of the people follows that of the prince, in the twentieth century we may take it that the religion of the prince, so far as it means anything constitutionally, will have to follow that of the people. If the whole population of this country were converted to Hinduism, the sovereign would certainly have to be a Hindu. In the present Babel, and the present atmosphere of (at least theoretical) religious tolerance, the natural arrangement is for the Queen to follow the historically appropriate branch of Christianity, as long as she does not make too much of it.

One aspect of the problem which is now commonly overlooked is the primitive role of religion as a means of binding a society together. Societies are bound by what they are bound by, not by what they ought to be bound by, and once there is serious competition between religious conceptions, none of them has a chance of being the binding force. One can understand why the deification of the Roman emperors, so absurd from our point of view, was proposed and finally accepted in a government which had extended itself to cover too many races and religions; and why when Christianity began to look like a winner, there was nothing for it but for the reigning emperor to take it over and make it the imperial religion. No form of this imperial solution is open to us. If there is, or is to be, a common religion, it can only be the religion of democracy, to which everyone more or less gives assent, and if it is not altogether understood by those who profess it, that is something it has in common with other religions. It has profound inadequacies – like the worship of the emperor – but like the worship of the emperor it can be practised side by side with another religion, except by persons of some scrupulosity or too much given to logic.

In a dim way, the Church of England perhaps understands

this. But it is in a dim way. The Church has conceived the notion of re-modelling itself in accordance with the more recent religion. An awful matiness is to replace Christian charity. A vulgar expression, designed not to add to the hearer's understanding, but to limit the Church's message to what the hearer already knows, has replaced the traditional language of Anglicanism, and with it both the rigour and the subtlety of its whole historical heritage. The aim evidently is to *substitute* the religion of democracy for the Christian religion. This naturally will not work, or if it does, people will no longer be Christians, whatever they call themselves. Even if success goes only so far as infiltrating the religion of democracy and attempting to overlay it with Christian meanings – rather as the Church in the early imperial centuries treated various pagan practices, giving them a Christian excuse – that will not work either. The religion of democracy is not a pre-Christian thing into which posterior meanings can be injected, but a post-Christian thing which is made up of Christian-derived elements gone slightly askew; it is a form of heresy, however amiable.

The only possibility is to accept the religion of democracy as the state religion in which Jews, Muslims, Hindus and others can also participate. This is not without its dangers for the state, as the uncivilized form of Christianity – Christianity, that is, before it had received its Roman education – was dangerous. Since the fundamental tenets of the democratic religion cannot be denied one should leave them as they are and content oneself with the *de facto* accretion of other elements, the most necessary of which is a profound respect for our local institutions and in particular for the government by the Queen in Parliament. Respect for the operations of this system has been eroded by the proliferation of international institutions which have their importance in their place but which are not to be regarded as alternative authorities.

The notion of a national religion, to which newcomers of all kinds can accede and which the native population more or less alienated from Christianity can recognize, is bound to be regarded as rather scandalous, and I do not propose to continue the argument beyond this point at the moment. I will however venture an Anglican comment. It is that the Church of England would in this conception of things, be free to be true to its historical mission as an 'unquestionably loyal' religious body which did not seek to influence governments except by bringing up Christians who would then exercise their own judgment in the affairs of the commonwealth. It would be free also to use the full measure of its riches – not least the Authorized Version and the Book of Common Prayer – to make a critical impact on the blowsy world of the late twentieth century, instead of aping the manners of that world as it seeks now to do. As for its traditional politics, they are not merely innocuous, they are manifestly favourable to the well-being of every man, woman and child in the country, whether of immemorial English stock or recently arrived from Central Europe or from Central Africa. Do they not centre – so far as this world is concerned, and this world is the world of politics – on the wish that the sovereign – the Queen in Parliament – should be granted 'in health and wealth long to live' and that she should be strengthened so as to 'vanquish and overcome all her enemies'? What citizen of the United Kingdom, with the minimum of benevolence towards the country, can wish for less?

# The Reverend Member?

THERE is good reason for thinking that Members of Parliament are not drawn from as wide a circle as they might be. There is no shortage of lawyers, company directors and trade union officials, nor of doctors and teachers of one sort and another. But that still leaves as virtual absentees many classes of persons who collectively know a lot about running what is now usually referred to as the economy. One class of persons who are entirely missing is the clergy of the Church of England. It cannot be said that their absence is the key to our present troubles, or even that it has been widely lamented. The clergy are, however, a special case, for it is against the law of the land for them to sit in the House of Commons.

We are happy to have a Synod always anxious to put things right. On the list of Private Members' Motions for the meeting next week (February 1982) there is one to be moved by the Archdeacon of Derby, which asserts 'That this Synod believes that clergymen of the Church of England should be free, like other citizens, to offer themselves for election as Members of Parliament' and seeks to move the Government 'to amend the relevant Act which forbids them to do so'. One should be astonished at nothing promoted in the Synod, and in this instance the author of the motion can point to the backing of a recommendation in the Church and State Report, 1970. There is a current case, supposed by some to be pathetic, of a clergyman who values his orders so little that he is laying them down, as far as in him lies, in order to circumvent the Act. This gentleman apparently feels that it is more important to be an MP than a parson – a point of view which, to say the least, does not display great unworldliness.

What would be the effect of this change in the law, if it were made? Not, one imagines, the flooding of the House of Commons with clergymen – the electors would see to that. It will be observed that the author of the motion has his eye on the liberty of the individual rather than on the well-being of the Church; what matters is that the clergyman 'should be free like other citizens'. Like most other citizens, it would have been better to say, for if the clergy are excluded by law as others are not, there are many whose employment and careers would be gone if they entered politics. What the Synod ought to be debating, surely, is not how free clergymen should be but whether the Church they serve would benefit from the proposed distractions. The legal exclusion is an oddity and there may be a case for removing it. What seems odder still is that the Synod should busy itself about this rather trivial matter before considering whether the Church needs clergy who are MPs.

The reason for the exclusion of the clergy seem to be lost in the mist. Blackstone thought that not having to serve in Parliament was originally regarded as one of the privileges of the clergy rather than as a restriction. Be that as it may, any question of removing the exclusion now will at once raise other questions of Church and State, notably that of abolishing such vestiges of the Establishment as remain. The political innocence of the reigning authorities of the Church of England, and of a large part of the membership of the Synod, is fabulous. Many who support the forthcoming Private Member's Motion will no doubt be delighted to see how much of the structure of the Establishment falls down when they touch it – and surprised a few years later to see how much harm they have done. There are Anglicans who think it wicked that they should have any privileges not shared by their non-conformist, including Roman, brothers. Rome no doubt agrees, as she proceeds quietly, with the help of the Foreign Office, to extend her own political influence, and for the moment rests on her laurels, having at last achieved a Papal Nuncio at the Court of St James's.

This step, whatever the arguments for it, can hardly be thought of as one towards equalizing the privileges enjoyed by the various ecclesiastical bodies at work in this country. It is, rather, a retrogression. If papal diplomacy were restricted, as on ordinary international proprieties it ought to be, to the affairs of a small Ruritanian state in Italy, there could be no possible cause for objection. But the Pope is a sadly mixed-up functionary, and his diplomats presume to speak on behalf of members of the Roman communion anywhere in the world. This not only amounts to giving the Roman Church an external diplomatic voice, and so an advantage not enjoyed by other ecclesiastical bodies; it goes clean against any democratic notion of government. Any diplomatic action on behalf of citizens of the United Kingdom should surely be taken by Her Majesty's representatives and by no one else. There is not a shred of support in constitutional theory, nor in the prevailing beliefs about the meaning of democracy, for any other view of the matter.

The current vein of self-immolation among Anglicans very likely appears to those concerned as a mark of spiritual purity. It is indeed a mark of Puritanism, which is not quite the same thing, though Puritans have always seen an affinity. An ecclesiastical structure cannot help having some sort of political existence. The Roman Church as the successor of the Roman Empire has always been aware of this, and has never ceased to meddle with the affairs of sovereign states. The post-Reformation English Church, in its heyday, had a delicate internal relationship with the state which kept it clear of the worst meddling; even so its privileges have been inexorably eroded because democracy cannot, in the end, admit any other appeal than to popular opinion. The papacy, like the monarch, is ultimately threatened by these tendencies. Both may survive a period of populism, but neither is founded upon populist principles. The monarchy we may have good hopes of, for it so to speak defines the terms of reference of our democracy and is the embodiment of its territorial reference and of a loyalty which is necessary for our survival.

The Papacy can look after itself, and it has on the whole done this, through the ages, by taking the political colour of the moment, as far as its lumbering steps allowed. Its untiring political encroachments have been slapped down time after time in the course of history. At the moment the Roman Church has what is, historically considered, an odd reputation as the champion of democracy in Poland; this must be largely the result of a series of events which has made it a centre of national feeling as it was in its former struggles against the Russian Orthodox Church. Politically, the motive of all Rome's politics may be said, without disrespect, to be its own survival and its own prevalence. The politics of present-day Anglicans have a childish look, in the face of such dignified and long-term objectives. To continue to chip away at the residue of the Establishment which the present arrangements are, without having anything to put in its place but a vague sentiment – that is not enough. No doubt a Church which has made light of the Book of Common Prayer and the Authorized Version must be thought to glory in its intellectual decline, but that sort of foolishness may after all not be a mark of sanctity but merely an insult to the intelligence of the Apostles.

Anyhow, when the Archdeacon of Derby rises to propose his motion in the Synod, he will have an opportunity of demonstrating that he understands that the Church of England does not exist in a political vacuum.

# The Archbishop's Travels

ONE could almost find it in one's heart to leave the Archbishop of Canterbury alone with his sorrows, as he awaits the Pope's visit. This little ecumenical occasion cannot be quite what he imagined. It may perhaps have the healthy result of bringing out differences which the authorities of the Church of England have been trying to smudge ever since they were given their head in 1974. However that may be, a church of so many alternatives should not be altogether surprised if some people are unable to see that a multiplicity of differences points infallibly to unanimity. Not all have been sanctified in the coffee-bars of Synod. But, however it may be with these high theological matters, there are more sordid considerations.

That the Pope should pay a pastoral visit to his followers in England is clearly something he may do if he wishes. One might think that he risks confusing himself as well as other people by his taste for travel, and that he might be better employed at home in the Vatican, but that is for him to judge. That he should, while he is here, exchange some civilities with the Archbishop of Canterbury, even with the Governor of the Church of England, is reasonable enough. That the visit should be made the occasion for meeting leaders of other denominations, in order, in his flying visit, to get a slightly less misleading picture of ecclesiastical dispositions in these islands, is also no bad thing.

It is surely rather puzzling, however, that the Archbishop should lay on simultaneous visits by heads of the Anglican communion overseas, as if he should wish to say, not exactly, 'My church is bigger than yours' – which he cannot say – but that he is not just the Archbishop of Canterbury but a bit of a traveller himself, with friends he can visit in other countries, and so cuts quite a figure in the world-wide Church of his aspirations.

Hasn't it all got rather out of hand? A disintegrated church at home is not healed by fixing its gaze on distant shores and the residual politics of post-imperial times. And the Pope surely, for all his talents, will have his work cut out to get even a plausible tourist's picture of this country during his short stay. He has been to Africa, he has been to South America, to the United States, to Ireland; he is always keen to pop home to see how things are going on in Poland. No doubt he has other jaunts in mind. Surely on this occasion he had better concentrate on the United Kingdom? It is a puzzling enough place for those of us who live here, and the airborne businessman, in less exalted lines of business, does not always take in all that he needs to be able to listen critically to the propositions of his branch managers.

If the Pope knocks over the furniture when he is here we shall have to pretend, out of courtesy to a distinguished foreign visitor, that he has not done so, or that it doesn't matter. We could even forgive our own archbishop if, in the heady atmosphere of a clerical get-together, he injudiciously laid on too large and too miscellaneous a party. It is a big occasion and it is not likely to happen again, in his time. But the truth is that this confusion between local and international affairs has become part and parcel of the office of Archbishop of Canterbury, as at present conceived. It is not too much to say that, as things are, the executive head of the Church of England is so preoccupied with his more far-flung collaborators that the Queen's realm of the United Kingdom is small beer to him. This natural preoccupation with the widest dimensions of Anglicanism is understandable enough, for what is more flattering than to be a World Figure? But it is a drawback for the Church of England, the historic entity to which the see of Canterbury has been related since the days of Augustine.

All the most notable developments in the Church of

England, in recent years, have been coloured, one might think excessively, by these international preoccupations. Of course there *are* international preoccupations, and someone has to attend to them, but even a good Foreign Secretary is not a substitute for a Prime Minister. The local sheep look up and are frankly puzzled. We like to hear about foreign parts, but we have our own parts. They have been left to wither. That is not how the Archbishop and those who aid and abet him would put the matter. But in fact, we have seen our Prayer Book thrown away, our superb version of the Bible demoted to a position of no importance, and a new sectarianism, which looks only to its own members, sweep over the parishes. Of course it is all in the name of holiness, like every other iniquity carried out in the name of the Church over the centuries – including the centuries before the sixteenth.

Let us pay no attention to holiness – or none to claims to it. It is, really, not the Anglican way. But now, one might say in all churches, not only in our own, the folly of sanctimonious claims knows no bounds. The degradation of current conceptions may be compendiously studied on the BBC's Sunday programme (at 8.15 am every week on Radio 4). In this ramshackle collection of what passes for religious news, not a week passes but some more or less ill-informed person is put up to say, with no authority whatever, that 'the church' thinks this or that about some fashionable event of the day. Politicians may be worried but, bless my soul, Christians know the answers! It is no sillier than some other programmes but it takes all the prizes for pretentiousness – unless, of course, one treats theological pretensions with complete contempt. One might suppose this to be the object of the organizers of the programme, but in fact one hardly believes them capable of such duplicity.

What is the local shepherd doing? Encouraging all this, as far as one can make out. It is, in fact, a natural outcome of the deliquescence of the Church of England, of which the abandonment of the Prayer Book has been more than a symptom. Bandaging their eyes and holding out their flabby hands as far as they would go, the leaders of the Church of England have exhorted its poor browbeaten members to avert their eyes from their duty in the commonwealth of the United Kingdom and to join in whatever wild-goose chases are proposed for the improvement of other people. It is not that some of these causes are not as deserving of support as political causes are likely to be, but that the miscellaneous spokesmen who claim our adherence to them because we are supposed to be Christians have no special competence to judge of these matters. The largest element of competence required is generally to be well-informed, which in a world buzzing more than ever with half-baked rumours it is extremely hard to be. Another element is that members of the Church of England have a duty of loyalty no less than other people; if our leaders think otherwise, they have changed the character of our church without authority and without telling us.

It has long seemed to me that, with the loosening of constitutional ties which has followed the dissolution of the Empire and entry into the Common Market, England stands at a disadvantage as compared with other components of the United Kingdom – with Scotland, Wales, even Ulster, though that is a more dubious case. I prefer England to the late Empire, and I should like it to survive. But whereas the other components expect to be reckoned with separately, England has to make do not only with the institutions but the personality of the United Kingdom. We are supposed to like to be smothered. With the Church of England it is even worse. We are blotted out under the Anglican robes of the Archbishop. Why not promote him to the role of Pope (new style) in the Anglican International, and give us an archbishop who could keep his mind on England?

Admittedly this proposition has become more difficult now, with the publication of the report of the Anglo-Roman Commission. A 'universal primacy' sits better with a notion of national churches, holding all Christians in a particular territory, than with a gaggle of churches of opinion each scattered across the world and making for more or less disruption. But that would mean a universal diminution of the authority of Rome, and the assertion of the primacy of Canterbury over Westminster.

# The Politics of David Hume *

IT would be an exaggeration to say that when David Hume, at the age of 26, came back to London after his retreat at La Flèche, he had already thought all the thoughts he was going to think. On the other hand, there is a sense in which the famous Hume, who lived among the learned and judicious in Edinburgh so comfortably and, one might say, so smugly in his eighteenth-century way, was a superfluity. True, he had still to write the *Enquiries,* the *Essays* and the *History of England,* but his crucial thoughts were contained in the *Treatise of Human Nature,* which fell still-born from the press and was not resuscitated in his lifetime, and that work had been completed at La Flèche. The rest was a gloss, an attempt, at least as successful as such things usually are, to get his novel ideas into the thick heads of his contemporaries. Our heads also being somewhat thick, that is not to say that we can afford to neglect the later works and the many explanations, illustrations and applications they offer. But Hume shared that characteristic which is perhaps even more marked in philosophers and scientists than in the rest of the world, of concentrating his inventions in the early part of his life.

One might think of this pattern of development as being less applicable to Hume's political thought than to his more radical principles. In a manner this is so, for the development of his political thought required more knowledge of the world than a studious young man could have time for, but the third book of the *Treatise,* entitled 'Of Morals', contains the core of his politics and, as David Miller is careful to demonstrate, the

* David Miller, *Philosophy and Ideology in Hume's Political Thought* (Clarendon Press)

epistemology and the politics are all of a piece. 'Bertrand Russell,' as Miller says, 'used [Hume] to illustrate the absence of any necessary connection between epistemological and political views, claiming to agree very largely with Hume in abstract matters while disagreeing totally with his politics.' Russell himself would be a better illustration of there sometimes being a wide disconnection between the two kinds of thinking, his own liberal fantasies being promulgated with the prestige rather than the reasonings of a philosopher. What Russell and Hume had in common, apart from the radical acuteness which was their genius, was a deficiency of interior life, as manifested in their works, which gives those works a certain imaginative poverty. One has only to compare Hume with his contemporary Johnson or his predecessor Berkeley to see his deficiency in this respect. If Hume was a somewhat comic, not to say stuffy figure, it was on account of these limitations. He became a Scotch gentleman of a very self-satisfied Edinburgh, having been a ruthlessly self-critical young man with scurvy spots on his fingers and wind in his stomach.

David Miller has lucidly separated 'the philosophical and ideological elements in Hume's political thought'. He follows the philosophical clues to the point at which they establish 'the terms on which Hume's thinking about politics' is conducted. He is able to show how limits are set to 'the kind of argument that can be produced in politics' – limits which people who have argued about politics since Hume have none the less continued to exceed. In our own scientific days, politicians and publicists, to say nothing of the intellectually, if not morally docile masses, never tire of assumptions and assertions which have no foundation either in reason or in experience. For Hume, 'if political arrangements were not wholly arbitrary, the reason was that men as a matter of fact imagined and felt in similar ways'. No doubt it could be asserted that that is a sort of empirical basis, though a shaky one. It is not, however, the basis on which utilitarianism, in its various manifestations, rests. Hume's account of moral judgment recognizes, as any realistic account must surely do, personal qualities which make no contribution to the general welfare, in any ordinary understanding of that term. This is the more impressive because he stands right outside the religious element in the Western tradition, which allows a continual interplay between worldly and otherworldly considerations: for Hume, religion is little but superstition and enthusiasm – an inadequate account, on any showing, but his rigour in this respect helps to give definition, if not definitiveness to his thinking.

The ideological components in Hume's political thought may be taken – as Miller takes them – to start with 'his conception of human nature, about which he held a view midway between the pessimism of, say, Hobbes and the optimism of, say, Rousseau or Godwin'. In Miller's excellent phrase, the postulate is the 'limited or partial benevolence' of mankind – a phrase which surely corresponds to what most of us think we have observed in ourselves and in others. As it is filled out, the conception is seen to contain more local traits. An interesting point, in relation to our present discontents, is Hume's observation that 'commerce is apt to decay in absolute governments not because it is there less *secure,* but because it is less honourable' – desire for social standing counting more with people than love of gain; it may well be that egalitarianism could produce the same results. In general, Hume's outlook on society is very much that of a man well content with the position of the upper classes in his day and with the degree of progress which recommended itself to them.

With this ideology, and what Miller calls the 'mitigated scepticism' of his less desperate philosophical positions, Hume's practical stance in politics did not differ in essentials from that of Burke or Adam Smith, although the situations and preoccupations of each of the three made for slightly different emphases. A significant point is that Hume died in 1776, and so before the enlightened talk of the Encyclopédistes had turned to blood. The less noticeable homicides of Hume's world consisted mainly in the hanging of a large number of criminals among whom there was perhaps more than a fair proportion of what he referred to as 'the meanest slaving poor'. The French Revolution certainly marked the end of the blandness in political reasoning which characterized the eighteenth century and of which Hume had his share.

The central question of political order is the question of allegiance, which, it is true, comes in many disguises – never more so than in our own day, which has a rich supply of cant words to confuse and indeed conceal the issue. One does not have to be an adherent of Mr Paisley to know that he is right to make an absolute distinction between those who accept the duty of obedience to the magistrate and those who do not – if wrong in the theological excuses he offers for something less than complete obedience on his own part. The problem of tenderness towards people manifestly disloyal raises its head also on the mainland of the United Kingdom, though happily not sharply as yet. There has been trouble with some who have taken great care that their disloyalty should not become manifest, or who have taken cover under a more or less open ambiguity. Of course those countries are happiest where such questions can be kept in the background, because more or less everybody is content with the constitutional arrangements and the dispute is only about policies, as has largely been the case here for the last three hundred years. It is possible to become too sleepy, however, as some notorious events uncovered in recent years have shown. There is the even more disquieting possibility that, in a society in which nothing is sacred except individual opinion, the very notion of the overriding claims of government may be lost. One need go no further than the Conservative Party itself, which has slid so far away from historic Toryism that many of its members think any intervention of the state is the work of the devil. Beyond that, and ultimately more menacing, is the growth of the superstition which attributes a reckless infallibility to the result of a vote, which is an intelligent device but only within an appropriate constitutional framework. There is also the assumption, encouraged all the time by thousands of persons who now make a living out of exploitation of opinion, that any group or any individual has a right to its interests while government has no rights at all. The unanimity here of free-enterprise Conservatives and the numerous more emphatically disruptive groups should cause a little reflection.

Hume's arguments about the nature of allegiance demonstrate the uncertainty of this as of every other political conception, but only for the reason that the world is a highly uncertain place. His sentiment is that 'liberty, though a laudable passion, ought commonly to be subordinate to a reverence for established government'. And so it ought. As with the physical world, there is a continuing reality which we ought to believe in, as a matter of common sense, wherever our fine ideas may take us in moments of speculation. 'Custom, then, is the great guide of human life.' It is in fact our guide through all the changes, whether we like it or not. That is Hume's cold and sober equivalent of *la carita del natio loco,* which was Dante's attachment in politics in the first instance, and for several instances after that, even though it did not prevent him from conceiving wider references for government or from subsuming all his affections finally in a universal scheme. The tepid philosopher refused to raise his eyes so high, or rather, by nature thinking first in general terms, he none the less saw the practical need to bring his thoughts down to the specific. So there was nothing irrational in praising actions 'more highly when their beneficial results fell on those connected to us by ties of kinship or acquaintance': that was 'a feature of moral judgment which reason could not alter'. If 'our interest is always engaged on the side of obedience to the magistracy', it is our present magistracy, our present constitution, that he has in mind, because it is established. Better the devil you know than the one some enthusiast proposes to you. Hume distrusted all absolutes, and what he regarded as the excessive attachments of the Tories as much as excessive claims for liberty. Yet in practice and by temperament he was probably more against change than Berkeley, whose more lively interior life allowed him to hold in mind simultaneously a belief in passive obedience and imaginings of freedom Hume did not dream of. No wonder he thought of tarwater while Hume thought of backgammon. David Miller does not wander so far from his subject. But, by following Hume so closely, he demonstrates both the need for using our wits as far as we can and the impossibility of any rational or scientific politics.

# Fairfax's Tasso* and the Seventeenth Century

'DANTE was a bitter man who had seen hell; Tasso was a gentleman who had read about Jerusalem.' Tasso must have read about Jerusalem to some purpose, for Chateaubriand, standing within sight of the city, was impressed by the verisimilitude of his description. But Ford Madox Ford's throwaway sentence explodes like a bomb on *Gerusalemme Liberata*. In an age which admires Dante – often without reading him – the implied criticism may seem to have destroyed Tasso entirely. Not that people pay all that much attention to the critical pronouncements of Ford Madox Ford – less than they should, I would say: but this sentence is deadly because, neatly put, it at once confirms the prejudices of education of anyone brought up in the past fifty years or so, and contains a terrible truth which cannot be denied. It belongs to the same succession of judgments as Eliot's putting down of Charles Whibley with the squib 'a critic would not use so careless a phrase as "Tasso's masterpiece"'. In fact, a critic might well speak of 'Tasso's masterpiece', in the right context. It would indubitably be wrong to mention the work in the same breath as the *Divine Comedy*, but it is wrong to let a relative judgment take on the character of an absolute. The seventeenth century was not much given to reading Dante, which should be a warning of the ups and downs of even the greatest reputations. And for the seventeenth century, Tasso was important.

There must be a lot of people, with a fair acquaintance with

* Kathleen M. Lea and T. M. Gang (Editors), *Godfrey of Bulloigne: A Critical Edition of Edward Fairfax's translation of Tasso's Gerusalemme Liberata, together with Fairfax's Original Poems* (Clarendon Press)

the English literature of the seventeenth century, who have never actually read Fairfax's Tasso, though all of them will know the translator's name and will have dipped into the work or read extracts from it. This sort of nodding acquaintance does not take one very far, with a work of this kind. There were five or six editions in the nineteenth century, none of them often to be picked up now in second-hand shops; there was an edition by the Centaur Press in 1962, thought to be rather highly priced at £4.50. That leaves plenty of room for this new edition. One must add that, well-groomed and 'critical' though it is, it can hardly be said to be cheap at £55; one may hope that it will prepare the way for a more popular edition in the course of a few years.

*Godfrey of Bulloigne* first appeared in 1600; Edward Fairfax, an illegitimate son of the Yorkshire family to which Marvell's Fairfax belonged, was born about 1568, so the translation is the work of a young man. Edward seems to have been living with his old father, in Yorkshire, during the years when the work was done, looking after family affairs in a manner which – true to form in such cases – made for trouble when the legitimate son and heir came home. Some particulars of this squabble are given in the biographical part of the introduction to this volume. Of more interest to the reader is the fact that the translator was a man settled in an old-fashioned gentleman's establishment, far from the capital, Edward apparently having returned there from Clare Hall, Cambridge. The book he was to translate was not particularly old-fashioned – the latest thing from Italy in 1584 (completed there in 1575) and already spoken of by Spenser in 1589 at the same time as Homer, Virgil and Ariosto – another case of uncritical talk, Eliot might have said.

Edward Fairfax himself might well have lumped all these authors of epics together, following Spenser, and he might have compounded the confusion by adding Spenser himself to the list; and Dryden can still mention Tasso with Homer and Virgil. It was the perspective of the age. The seventeenth century had a notion of heroic poetry, and of narrative poetry merely, which has ceased to have operational force in our day. The 'long poem' for us – with Pound and MacDiarmid – is a rag-bag, and the sort of continuous writing in verse which was a central notion, and a not uncommon practice, in former times, is now probably a merely academic conception for most people. While one would not wish to provoke – God forbid – a spate of long narrative poems, it can be said that anyone whose reading has not included a number of such productions from past ages will have a very defective idea of the uses of verse. In the infancy of the novel people turned to the story in verse for a good read rather than for any of the more high-falutin reasons given by critics. This was certainly the case when Fairfax was writing, and the need was satisfied, in varying degrees, by Daniel and Drayton as well as by Spenser. The habit of writing histories and fictions in verse may be regarded as the fag-end of medieval and older traditions – of Chaucer to the Chansons de Geste and beyond.

The habit had its own Renaissance colouring. To the charm of the narrative was added – and nowhere more than in Spenser and Tasso – the charm of a curiously transmuted sentiment of chivalry, something which has only to be named to be found repugnant by most readers of the late twentieth century. Yet it is a very elementary error, for anyone to whom the pleasures of literature are accessible, to dismiss the work of another age because of the prejudices of this one. Superficial fashions of any kind soon show up for the tawdry affairs they always were, but what has appealed deeply to the minds of earlier generations will always be found, on closer acquaintance, to have meaning for our own; such discoveries are of the essence of humane studies or, more simply, of reading for pleasure in any extended way. There must be people who have been put off reading *The Faerie Queene* by *notions* of the sort of thing it is. Yet anyone who starts to read it without being too much bullied by our contemporary inhibitions will find himself drawn on by the clarity and elegance of a language very little obfuscated by its few quaintnesses, into a world certainly not less grown-up than our own.

Tasso must mean less to an English reader than Spenser, but in the translation of Fairfax *Gerusalemme Liberata* has been made so much at home here that it is, at the least, a piece of reading which anyone who cares for the core of our literature will find illuminating as well as pleasurable. As to the supposedly inaccessible sentiment, W. P. Ker, a voice from the early part of this century which admittedly may sound to some as remote at Tasso's, said: 'It is difficult to explain, but it is easy to recognize in the gravity and melancholy grace of Tasso something closely akin to the English conceptions of true valour and nobility in the first half of the seventeenth century.' True valour and nobility may seem to modern readers a small and elusive part of those times or of any other, but it is a perfectly genuine element in them none the less. Ker goes on to say: 'The religion of Tasso, in spite of all differences, was found acceptable by English readers; it is easier to understand than Milton's.' That points to something far more complex than a mere antithesis between Reformation and Counter-Reformation.

The qualitative difference between Tasso and Dante can hardly be better illustrated than by putting side by side the Ulysses of Canto XXVI of the *Inferno* and the miraculous voyage in the fifteenth canto of the *Gerusalemme*. It would be folly to expect the combination of intellectual and imaginative force of Dante, or his laconic expression, to be equalled. Who does equal them? Fifty lines of Canto XXVI give us the story, as against five hundred in Tasso, and with Dante we are so close to the roots of the human mind that the impression is not of legend but of reality. Yet Tasso's tale is far from negligible, and tells far more in a short space than most of the literature admired in our own time. Two Christian knights go in search of the hero Rinaldo. None of the ordinary difficulties of navigation are encountered, for their craft is charmed, and a reliable damsel goes with them. Starting from the Holy Land, where the First Crusade is in full swing, though with few marks of historical verisimilitude except the presence of Godfrey of Bulloigne himself, they sail westward along the North African coast, past Crete, past Rhodes, past where the 'pride and pomp' of Carthage 'lies in sand and grasse'. Passing the Pillars of Hercules, their guide recalls Ulysses:

> He past those pillours, and in open wave
> Of the broad sea first his bould sailes untwind,
> But yet the greedie Ocean was his grave...

Neither in Fairfax nor in his original is the terror, or the intelligence, of Dante's account approached. The Renaissance inhabits a more hopeful world, and after the recollections of Ulysses comes a prophecy of Columbus, not difficult for the poet of the sixteenth century. It is not Dante's 'mondo senza gente' that the party find as they run "twixt South and West', but the Canaries, mythologized, where Rinaldo lies enslaved in the most delightful way disapproved of by moralists. The sea closes over Dante's Ulysses, but the Crusaders return with the liberated hero to continue the battle for Jerusalem.

Fairfax never has Spenser entirely out of his mind as he renders Tasso's description of the Fortunate Isles and their delightful pitfalls. Indeed *Godfrey of Bulloigne* as a whole is unthinkable without Spenser, who no doubt set Fairfax on his way as a poet. But the translator was saved by his Italian original from the vices of the mere Spenserians. He had a simpler stanza form to manage – though he could not, of course, match the feminine rhymes of the Italian – and he had before him the superior clarity of a more mature language, which did not tempt him as he might otherwise have been tempted to over-long sentences. He must have been helped, too, by the comparative forthrightness of Tasso's narrative. Spenser no doubt owes more to Boiardo and Ariosto, and if Tasso is still episodic, he is much less so than Spenser – much less so than Virgil, Landor thought. Indeed Landor, who is to be taken seriously in such matters, considered the *'Gerusalemme Liberata*... of all such compositions, the most perfect in plan'. Admittedly, perfection of plan has its limitations, in a long poem of any kind, but there is in Tasso a sense of movement and direction towards the end which must have been helpful to the translator. Moreover Fairfax seems, on such evidences as we have, to have been an unpretentious man, and if like all translators he sometimes departs a little from his original, it is rarely in order to present the reader with something he thinks will be more impressive. While Spenserians such as Giles and Phineas Fletcher were going a way which lost itself in the sand, Fairfax hit one of the trails the language of his time was taking, towards a certain thinness, no doubt, but also towards a certain elegance, so that one can understand how it was that, as Dryden reports, 'our famous Waller' owned that 'he deriv'd the harmony of his numbers from *Godfrey of Bulloign*, which was turned into English by Mr Fairfax'.

There is plenty of neatness in Fairfax, of a kind which increased in English until it was overdone: 'Thus women know, and thus they use the guise,/T'enchant the valiant, and beguile the wise.' But there is no great air of contrivance about most of the verses. 'One would expect an epic to maintain a lofty level of style throughout', say the present editors, apparently without repugnance. 'Tasso maintains such a level, Fairfax does not.' The contemporary English reader is unlikely to complain. The translation holds our interest; and this is the first requisite in a long poem. It would be wrong to suggest that Fairfax has any exceptional powers of invention, but he gets the sense of the Italian into lively and convincing English:

> To all deceit she could her beautie frame,
> False, faire and yong, a virgin and a witch

stands for Tasso's

> gli accorgimenti e le più occulte frodi
> ch'usi o femina o maga a lei son note.

Fairfax can manage his stanza admirably and present a traditional topic with freshness and effect:

> So, in the passing of a day, doth pas
> The bud and blossome of the life of man,
> Nor ere doth flourish more, but like the gras

> Cut downe, becommeth withred, pale and wan:
> O gather then the rose while time thou hast,
> Short is the day, done when it scant began,
>> Gather the rose of love, while yet thou mast
>> Loving, be lov'd; embrasing, be embrast.

The English language at the turn of the sixteenth/seventeenth centuries was in a happy condition, and Fairfax had the gift of it. The editors, besides presenting us with a carefully prepared text of *Godfrey,* have usefully included what remains of Fairfax's original poems: if there is not great force, there is charm in his 'Epitaph upon King James' (presumably written more than a quarter of a century after the translation):

> All that have eyes now wake and weep;
> He whose waking was our sleep
> Is fallen asleep himself, and never
> Shall wake more till he wake ever.
> Death's iron hand has closed those eyes
> That were at once three kingdoms' spies....

Tasso's matter was entirely suitable to be made at home in Jacobean and Caroline England, and Fairfax did make it at home, which is surely the most a translator can be expected to do. The theme is an echo of older European concerns, distanced already in the Italian. For what was the First Crusade then in Ferrara? A dim recollection recalled by the battle of Lepanto (1571), or the anxieties raised by the fall of Constantinople (1453)? There is no realism in Tasso, as regards the nature of the enemy, and little in relation to other outward matters, for this is a world of sorcerers, maiden warriors, and other colourful paraphernalia. But the inward seriousness of the poem is not in doubt. If we treat with reserve the detail of the alleged allegory, there is still no question but that the work as a whole gives us the elements at war in the poet's grave and highly cultivated mind. The cause matters; beyond the taking of Jerusalem, a Christian salvation. Tancred says:

But beare me to this roiall towne, I pray,
That if cut short by humaine accident
I die, there may I see my latest day,
The place where Christ upon his crosse was rent....

(for Tasso's 'loco ove mori l'Uomo immortale'). In Fairfax's rendering we have the very stuff of seventeenth-century religious apprehension, from Donne to Bunyan.

The enemy, for the Counter-Reformation, was rather Protestants than Saracens, as for the English Puritans it was Prelates and the Great Whore of Babylon, and it is this unprepossessing struggle which is caught up in Tasso's epic, for if he had 'read about Jerusalem', he had seen the Counter-Reformation at closer quarters. How little any poet – or perhaps anyone else – gets beyond his time! There is no doubt more of the impetus which inspired the First Crusade in *La Chanson de Roland* than there is in the *Gerusalemme Liberata,* of which it is the nominal subject. *Roland* was probably composed about the time of Godfrey's capture of Jerusalem, and it falsifies its own nominal subject, the Pyrenean campaign of Charlemagne, to a tale of imperial Christian armies wiping the floor with the Saracens. There is no end to the sleight-of-hand of poets, or to human misunderstanding.

# A Word of Apology

THE POLITICS expressed or implied in my writings have been the subject of so much misunderstanding – some of it, one must suppose, wilful – that I think I should try to set down at least what they do *not* amount to. The materials for a *positive* understanding of what I have said are to hand in *The Avoidance of Literature* (1978) and *The Spirit of British Administration*, (1959, 2nd edn 1966). It would be something if here one could remove a few of the confusions current among those who impute to me attitudes and designs which are unlike any I ever took or entertained.

An initial difficulty is the sense of the word *politics*. In terms of the policies most loudly discussed and disputed about – the matter of party programmes and the like – I have nothing directly to offer. The concern which has permeated so much of my writing, and given it such political content as it has, is for something different. It is a long-standing obsession with the *res publica*. What attitudes towards it promise least damage to the things I most care for? If that seems too personal a question, in relation to so large a subject, one can only ask what other question anyone can ask. One difficulty of an enquiry on this basis is that one cannot enumerate the things one does most care for. To attempt to do so at all one would have to have more faith than I have in the capacity of half-a-dozen much talked-of abstractions.

When Johnson said that patriotism was the last refuge of the scoundrel he was speaking with his customary succinctness and irony, and the gloss on it is to be found in his Dictionary, where two meanings are given to the word 'patriot':

1 One whose ruling passion is love of his country.
2 It is sometimes used for a factious disturber of the government.

One does not have to lay any claim to a particular civic virtue to take the sense of the distinction. Most of the great words currently used in politics have an analogous ambivalence, and it is for this reason that they are best avoided. Politics are not, in fact, about such words, although a high proportion of political discourse is about little else; they are about the elusive substance after which these words only grope. Rhetoric is part of the mechanics of politics – never absent, for it is always necessary to persuade people to follow courses they only imperfectly understand. In an age of wide political publics and of a language sorely tried by commercial and other demagogic uses, it occupies a grotesquely large part of the public field. All the more need for enquiries which operate below the demagogic level and are concerned with what really happens, what *is*. In fields of technology and business (public or what is called private) such enquiry is a matter, initially or intermediately, for experts, and no one in his senses will form a view on practical matters of any complexity without hearing what experts have to say. But there is an irreducible field of determination, the meeting-point of expertises and passions – including the passions of experts – which is the field of ordinary discourse and so of politics. There, one is in the realm of attitudes and orientations which aspire to the rank of knowledge without ever entirely making good their claims. They do not do so because they involve those intractable truths about the nature of man which everyone supposes to be there, whether they appoint a god or some material law as the keeper of the explanation.

It is in this uncertain realm that all theories of politics have their roots, whether or not they like it and whatever their claims. The demand for vulgarization inseparable from the practice of politics is such that the final uncertainties do not get the credit they deserve. In practice, one has to turn aside from mere belief, or for what sometimes passes as an alternative to belief – mere assertion – to seek for more accessible bases for a political theory. If only one could find a *fact* to rest upon! The solution is generally found, in these days, in facts so numerous as to conceal from those who propose them the uncertainty of the orientation by which they have been found. If one admits that uncertainty, one has to confess that any choice of a starting-point is arbitrary. The starting-point cannot be justified; it can only be loved. The admission of this pathetic reality not only disarms the proponent but puts him at risk from anyone who points out that a starting-point so chosen has an inconvenient affinity with the vulgarest tools of rhetoric. That affinity, it seems to me, one cannot deny; but an affinity is not an identity and on that perhaps unimpressive distinction one can take one's stand.

It is not unilluminating to point to a formulation by one who has gone as far as any contemporary in recommending the dissolution of everything – the Roumanian E. M. Cioran:

> 'Prejudice' – for we are in the world of prejudices – 'is an organic truth, false in itself, but accumulated through generations and transmitted: you cannot get rid of it with impunity. The people which gives it up without scruple disowns itself again and again until there is nothing left to disown. The duration and consistency of a collectivity coincide with the duration and consistency of its prejudices.'
>
> *Précis de décomposition*, 1949, ed. 1977 p. 166.

These prejudices must include all those to which rhetorical appeal can be made. In reality, people do not free themselves from prejudice; they merely change one agglomeration for another – and that with less facility than is usually imagined. The stubbornness of inherited prejudice is concealed to some extent by the linguistic evolutions which, for example, translate a theological into a political notion, or vice versa, or account for a social change in language which was formerly used for another. The persistence of prejudice – often denounced by people who themselves illustrate the process to perfection – is so far from being entirely nefarious that without it we should hardly be able to talk to one another at all. A basis of common pre-conception is necessary for any interchange of thought and it is one of the popular delusions of our time that discourse across cultural barriers of a more or less mountainous kind must be more fruitful than the refinements which arise only in the intercourse of more or less homogeneous groups. There are elements of both kinds of discourse in that study of the past which is an inseparable part of literary studies, and it is for this reason that literature has been, is and is likely to be, the basis of any humane education.

It is possible to object to the *vérité organique* which persists from generation to generation, and it is a function of philosophy to take exception to this form of truth. Neither objection nor critical examination can, however, be made without invoking a number of truths of no better pedigree. But whether philosophers or not, we all inhabit the world of eating and drinking and so belong to the *res publica* in which we eat and drink. Nobody is in a position to make any difficulty about that proposition, but when it comes to defining the *res publica* the clash of hereditary prejudice begins to be ferocious. It is in fact often more ferocious than it need be, for we are here in the realm of fact. The facts, however, are so numerous that to assemble even a few people to examine small concentric or even over-lapping groups of them can be gruesomely difficult. There are, roughly speaking, two ways of looking at political theory. There is the method of those who know, *a priori*, the nature of the universe, and so start from the whole and have to strain their eyes to see what is under their noses; and there are those who admit to inheriting a number of prejudices and are short-sighted enough to see mainly the facts before their faces. The former category includes those who have inherited the systematic mania of certain nineteenth-century philosophers and who therefore claim to see the whole wood whether or not they can make out particular trees. This is now a commonplace among many whose own methods of thought have remarkably little of the systematic or even of the rational about them. There is hardly a tyro of politics who does not start from various bald assertions about 'society' as if he saw the whole thing in the palm of his hand. The second category comprises those who are relatively free from the obfuscations deriving from general theory and see the world piece-meal, and in their better moments claim only to see the pieces before their eyes. It goes without saying that these characterizations of the two categories are approximate and a little partial, but they may serve to indicate the kind of perspective I think is desirable for the approach to political theory. I regard myself as belonging to the second category – to those incapable of taking a grand view of collective behaviour.

Of course, if one manages to detach oneself from the worst trammels of omniscient theory, and to fix one's eyes on the proper object of political studies – historical, including actual, institutions – one may still be confused by their multiplicity. Even if one should renounce all but the immediate past and look around one, it is confusing enough. Does one start at home and fix one's eyes on the District Council or even the Parish Council? Does one lift up one's eyes to the County Borough or County Council? All these more or less neological forms have their charm. Or does one stare with glazed eyes at the various supernational organizations which have more or less of the character of governments – the EEC or the United Nations? Well, perhaps. But it is hardly an eccentricity to look principally at the government of the United Kingdom and, if one happens to belong to England, either through unidentified generations or as a newcomer, it is not unreasonable – and should not be repugnant to one's affections – to look particularly at the English roots of our current institutions and prejudices. This is the nature of my interest in these matters. The constitutional quarrels of the seventeenth century have a bearing on the arguments of today, and if I have emphasized one side in the old dispute it is because the sense of it has so almost entirely disappeared from view that contemporary discussions are conducted in ignorance of it. A restatement in modern terms is necessary if our reflections are to be nourished from the past as they should be: We do not escape from the past by not understanding it, for it is the main source of our ideas and habits. The question is not whether we take from the past, but whether we take from it with or without reflection.

There are people who think that one should not entertain unfashionable ideas at all. The prohibition is hardly a form of liberalism. The danger of anyone reinstating the Caroline world is not what one could call imminent. When I gave an account of Toryism in *PNR 1* I expressly characterized it as 'an obscure... opposition', adding that it was 'ill-understood' – which has been abundantly illustrated since. The real difficulty of those who purvey this incomprehension is, in Cioran's terms, that they think that this realm of England should 'renounce without scruples' the prejudices which are the root and growth of its continuance; should go on disowning itself 'until there is nothing more to disown'. It is an invitation which will hardly appeal to the literate, even if they think, as I do, that one should not encourage the development of a deliberately national culture. We cannot renounce the past of England as long as its literature continues to live for us. Of course, since the English language is now used so widely, it is properly disrupted all the time by people having their primary attachments elsewhere. But that does not suggest to me that we who are here should abandon our past. A better conclusion would be that we should not assimilate parrot-like what comes to us from outside, but so accost it that what we take in we take in without breaking the continuum of our own thoughts.